Brothers

Brothers

the editors of Esquire

HYPERION

New York

Library of Congress Cataloging-in-Publication Data

ISBN 0-7868-6520-2

Book design by Claudyne Bianco Bedell

First Edition
10 9 8 7 6 5 4 2 3 1

Contents

Acknowledgments

Brothers got its start, as most good ideas do, over dinner. *Esquire* writers Scott Raab, Cal Fussman, and Tom Junod and I all found ourselves in New York on the same day and ended up in some *rodizzio*, eating charred meat and (except for Scott) drinking *capirinhas*. We were talking about future photographic portfolios for the magazine and someone—we can't remember who—mentioned the word *brothers*. We started imagining pictures of pairs of brothers, and we could see that each photo would tell its own story—about love or conflict, about rivalry or friendship.

Through magic, inspiration, and a whole bunch of hard work on the part of *Esquire*'s staff, that conversation eventually became a special issue of *Esquire* magazine. To make the considerable leap from magazine to book, we turned to *Esquire* senior editor Jay Woodruff. Working with deputy photography editor Ian Spanier and freelancer Neil Giordano, Jay not only took full advantage of many of *Esquire*'s regular contributors but added the work of some of our country's most distinguished writers and photographers.

Brothers would not have happened without Jay. And while he deserves an enormous amount of credit, his wife Sarah and their kids, Joe, Sam, and Annie, also deserve thanks for putting up with his many late nights at the office.

—David Granger, editor-in-chief, *Esquire*

Foreword
David Granger

When I think of my brother, Mark, I think of someone who can do anything, fix anything, build anything.
I think of him as patient and compassionate and determined. I think of him as being at peace in the
world. But mostly, I marvel at how he understands the way things work. Mark once bought a wrecked
Austin-Healey from a friend of mine, remade it from bonnet to boot, and sold it for many times his pur-
chase price. At the time, I don't think he was actually old enough to drive. He, like our father, is entirely undaunted by tasks. We once spent a summer together—Mark and I and a jack-of-all trades named E.
L. Reynolds—assigned the task of building a dwelling on some lake property we'd owned for a decade. I
looked at the empty lot and the mounds of building materials and saw an empty lot and mounds of building materials. Mark saw a house. Mark always was and still is firm in his faith that the world of things
will bend to his will.

I am not that way. And I suspect that we recognize in our brothers the traits that make us different more than we do the traits that make us similar. We may have the same ears, the same crooked
front teeth, remarkably similar speech patterns. But precisely because of our similarities, we struggle
through much of our lives to prove that we're different from this thing that's been forced upon us.
Brothers tend to battle for every small victory—Dad's praise, Mom's meatloaf, room enough to breathe.

We grow up in rivalry and define ourselves, in part, by how distinct we are from the person or persons closest to us. As you look at the photographs in this book, I suspect you'll find yourself as struck by the differences as by the likenesses. And if there is a thread that runs through the stories we've gathered here, it is that we can feel so connected to a man we define in large part precisely by how dissimilar from us he is.

It's a surprisingly complicated relationship, brotherhood— admiration and resentment, dependence and rivalry all mixed up together. And, strangely, as fundamental as it is to us, it may be the easiest relationship in our busy, complicated lives to take for granted. It's our hope that in this book—in the amazing photographs and the compelling stories—we give our brothers their due.

Introduction

TOBIAS WOLFF

When men talk about their brothers, the stories are too often regretful, and sometimes bitter; youthful rivalry persisting unabated into later years, with no end in sight; resentments over the treatment of a wife; the exploitation of a parent's unequal affection; a loan gone bad; feuds so old their causes are forgotten, or too painful to speak of. It is a bitter thing to be divided from your brother. All that makes for closeness, when it goes wrong, also makes for suspicion and rancor. I have a brother myself, and I know how easily things can go wrong. We weren't always as careful as we should have been, Geoffrey and I. We tried each other, naturally. So it's in gratitude, not in pride, that I look back and see that between us things did not go wrong, and that the very moments when our brotherhood was most in danger have become our redemption narratives—the grenade that didn't go off, the flood that never quite reached the rooftop, the terrible crash we walked away from.

This is the story of one of those crashes.

When I was fifteen I took a Greyhound from Seattle to La Jolla to spend the summer with

Geoffrey Wolff, 61, and Tobias Wolff, 53, writers

Photographed by Jeff Dunas in Los Angeles, California, December 12, 1998.

my father and brother. This was June, 1961. I hadn't seen my father since 1954, and didn't recognize him when he finally showed up, alone, two hours late, to pluck me from the crowd of sailors and grifters and dirty old men cruising the bus station. His face was bloated and jowly. He was driving a green sports car. He'd been drinking and was nervous with me, and as we drove away from the station he said he wanted to stop by his fiancée's. *Fiancée?* I was whipped—it was well after midnight—but he insisted. The house was dark when we arrived, and my father had to lean on the bell before she came to the door in her bathrobe and let us in. He had a couple of drinks and picked a fight with her and she threw us out. The next day they made it up, and the day after that the two of them headed off to Las Vegas.

May I say that I was a little confused? The idea, as I'd understood it from my father's phone calls, was that he and Geoffrey and I would join up and have some fun together until I left for boarding school in the fall. My brother was the big draw. We hadn't laid eyes on each other in seven years, but we'd exchanged letters and stories, and he'd guided me through my applications for a scholarship to prep school. I was sharply disappointed not to find him in La Jolla when I arrived, and now my father was gone too.

He came back from Vegas a week later minus the sports car—which he'd burned up in the desert—on the outs with his fiancée and about to lose his job at Convair Astronautics for missing work. It became clear to me that I didn't know the man and couldn't count on him. He was hitting the sauce. Sober, he was good company. Drunk, he turned ugly and raged against those who'd disappointed him—my God, who hadn't? This went on night after night. And then my brother arrived.

I will never forget the sight of Geoffrey stepping down off that bus. He wore a rumpled seersucker suit. He looked bone-tired and needed a shave. Though I spotted him right off, he was not the boy I'd known, not the boy I thought of when I wrote my letters and when I said, testing the words, not quite believing them, "My brother . . . " He was twenty-three now, a college graduate. He had the aspect of a man on his own in a foreign country, a cultivated detachment that struck me even then as literary, and romantic. But when he came up to me and took my hand, I saw in his face the plain wish for friendship, and I could have wept with relief.

My father hit bottom that night. He'd gone out to buy us some steaks and never returned. Geoffrey and I were wakened by a call from his fiancée. It turned out he'd been at her place, where he'd suffered a complete breakdown, speechlessness, paralysis, the works. The police got involved and found a number of warrants for his arrest—speeding, bad checks, grand-theft auto . . . it turned out that one of the bad checks was for the sports car he'd destroyed. They took him "downtown" but he was obviously non compos mentis, so justice deferred to compassion and he was forwarded to Buena Vista Sanitarium, where he was to remain for most of the summer.

Mind you, this all happens on the very night Geoffrey pulls into town. Within hours. And I thought *I* was disappointed!

This is Geoffrey's situation. He has just graduated from Princeton, no mean feat considering he's had to come up with the money himself since the end of his first year there, when my father split from his rich wife and she stopped coughing up the tuition. Geoffrey had sweated his way through, with a good boost from his earnings at poker, and still managed to distinguish himself as a young critic and earn the favor of teachers like Richard Blackmur, Walt Litz, George Steiner.

Graduating summa cum laude, he'd been offered a teaching job at Robert College in Istanbul, and with that prospect he had mapped out a pretty agreeable summer for himself, sailing the New England coast with a buddy (on the buddy's father's yacht) while preparing his lectures for the coming semester. What dreams he must have had—college friends greeting him in every port with foaming magnums of bubbly, girls swooning to his understated tales of life on the deep, then back to the swelling canvas and the heavy, beautiful books.

Then the old man (Geoffrey's name for him, henceforth mine) calls him, just before he sets sail, and issues a summons to La Jolla for the summer. Hah! Fat chance. The last time they were together was when the old man sold a collection of Revere silver he'd stolen from his wife to pay Geoffrey some dough he owed him. So Geoffrey wasn't inclined. Then the old man played his trump. Toby will be here, he said.

Now why that should have been a strong card is almost beyond me. Geoffrey was a young man. I was still a kid. We'd never been very close, not even before our parents took us to opposite ends of the country eleven years back. Lately there'd been some warmth between us through the mail, but come on. The sailboat. The friends. The rolling seas and creak of the stays, the Shakespeare and Marlowe and Auden and Johnson and James . . .

Toby will be here, the old man said. Okay, Geoffrey said, and said good-bye to his shipmate, and rode the Hound across the country.

It doesn't make sense. For years I've wondered at his decision, wondered most of all if I'd have done the same thing in his place. He knew the old man well enough to figure that the plan wouldn't hold up; that there'd be a mess to deal with soon enough (though he couldn't have guessed how soon). Aside from the sailing, he had a pile of work to get done before September. There was no profit for him in this move, no benefit that I can imagine save one, the satisfaction of the desire to know and befriend his brother. I can imagine it because I felt it myself. But it didn't cost me anything, and it cost him plenty.

Here he is, then, in a strange town with a brother he barely knows. The support he's been promised will not be forthcoming. The landlord has served notice of eviction for non-payment of rent—several months' worth. So what can Geoffrey do? He can send the kid back to Washington State and hop another bus going east. That's the obvious choice. But again, he does it the hard way. First he goes out to Convair Astronautics and gets himself a job turning technical manuals into English, the same job the old man had; maybe that's why there was an opening. Then he buys a car. Then he finds us another apartment and puts me on a serious schedule of reading and writing. In short, he becomes the father in this family.

Why? It wasn't for the pleasure of my company. I was ignorant and lazy, magnificently unprepared for the rigors of the school I'd be going to. I meant well, in a non-committal way, but I had crooked habits, not unlike the old man's, and these soon made themselves evident in ways that challenged Geoffrey's good will and still give me shame to recall. And yet I imagine that he stayed on not in spite of these deficits of mine, but partly because of them, seeing how much help I needed if I was to survive, let alone prosper, in the new life ahead of me.

Every three or four days I had to produce an essay on an assigned text. I liked to read, but these books, his treasures, were new to me. Greek plays, essays by Camus, novels by Fitzgerald and Faulkner. *King Lear*. The essay topics might sound a little funny now, highly serious, even owlish, and touching in Geoffrey's ambition for me, but they forced me to think about metaphor, and ambiguity, and language as an end in itself. This concern with language extended to the spoken word. He taught me to say "get" instead of "git," and that the final participial "g" is *not* silent. There were questions of style to be addressed: it seemed that where I was going, boys did not wear their hair swept back into DAs; they did not wear blue jeans low on their hips or belt buckles to the side, or roll packs of Kools into the sleeves of their T-shirts. I caught his love of jazz and jokes and—alas for me—unfiltered Camels. In return I taught him the songs of Hank Williams, whose oeuvre I had by heart.

On Sundays we drove all over creation to get to the sanitarium, where the old man had set himself up as lord of the resident ironists who believed themselves to be more sane than their doctors. He always had a circle of them around him in the lounge when we came to visit, nodding agreement as he ridiculed the entire head-shrinking enterprise. It wasn't altogether amusing. I could sense that Geoffrey was more worried they'd let the old man out than that they'd keep him in. He had his hands full with work, and paying bills, and dealing with me, and trying, with discouraging results, to steal enough time and clarity of thought to prepare his classes. The strain told, on both of us.

Those few months changed me. Of course I mean something other than the grooming I got, which indeed proved not just valuable but essential. But until that summer I'd never known anyone who lived for ideas and words; to whom writing, his own and others', was not a diversion from life but an imperative form of life. Ever since I was eleven or twelve I'd written tales of mystery and horror and adventure, and had notions of being an "author," but after that summer I never really wanted to be anything else. Week after week of breathing the incense of respect for sentences and stories helped bring me to the judgment, right or wrong, that there was no better way to spend my life than in making them. Maybe I would have been a writer anyway. Who knows what he'd have done but for this or that experience? I do know that my brother's conviction of the supreme value of writing something good helped give my own attempts the character of a quest rather than a career, which was damned lucky for me, because seen as a career it would've been frustrating beyond my power to endure.

So here was a lasting gift my brother fashioned from the wreckage of that summer. But in the end it wasn't his material support or his intentional lessons that meant most to me, or even his vocational inspiration, but the abiding knowledge that I had a brother who would act against his own immediate interests on my behalf, not just on impulse but day after day.

I've never asked Geoffrey exactly why he came, or why he stayed. At the time it didn't occur to me to ask. He was there; that was enough. Later on I tried to imagine the reasons, as I've done here, but still without asking, because what he did had an unconsidered, instinctual quality that shouldn't have to explain itself, and probably couldn't. It runs counter to reason, as the world reasons. It answers only to the economy of brotherhood, whose accounting practices defy and embarrass the world's.

What a shambles of a summer it was, though, and how we love to remember it—the essay topics . . . the golden girls who snubbed us on Wind and Sea Beach . . . the party the old man took us to when he got out, all of the guests fruitcakes he'd known in Buena Vista . . .

That's one crash we lived to tell about. There were others. But it's time to yield the floor. The good luck of having a brother is partly the luck of having stories to tell—stories like the ones that follow.

naughty, awful boys

Larry Doyle

My mother tells this story. I'm about four and my brother, Kevin, is two. One morning we get up early, hungry. My mother awakes to the sound of squealing. She walks into the kitchen and discovers the two of us taking turns pushing each other across a linoleum floor thickly oiled with the insides of a couple dozen eggs.

If I close my eyes, I can see my brother and me: laughing, slippery, sticky. I see myself steering him around by the head, sliding him giggling into a clatter of pots and pans; I can see my own face, a long droop of yolk hanging off my chin. That's how I know I have no memory of it.

One time, when my brother and I were home from college, he got drunk and shoved me into the wall. *I should beat the shit out of you*, he said, his forearm across my chest. *You used to pound me all the time, I remember, man. You'd sit on me and you'd pound my arm, keep pounding, in the same place. Pounding. You'd just keep pounding, pounding, and I couldn't get up.*

I'm pinned there, thinking, *Could've happened.* But it hadn't made any lasting impression on me.

I do remember this: I was pounding my brother this other time, and he got away from me and managed to scamper under the kitchen nook. I had him by the ankle and was dragging him out when my mother walked in. Naturally, I let go. But my mother said, *No, don't let me stop you. Go on and kill your brother for all I care. Go on.* She began slapping the back of my head, shoving me toward my brother, curled into the corner, knees to chest. *He's your brother; you want to kill him, kill him. Go on, beat him up. Beat him up—you want to.*

I began to cry. I no longer wanted to pound my brother so much as I wanted to hug him. But he wouldn't come out.

I wonder if he remembers that.

My parents were always threatening to send us to the "awdy" home. At the time we thought the awdy home was just the name for the place bad boys went, some boogey stew of naughty and awful; in fact it was the Arthur J. Audy Home for Children, now known less evocatively as the Cook County Juvenile Temporary Detention Center. The threat was usually conditional—*If you keep that up . . . one more stunt like that*—and therefore empty, but then one winter night my parents got us out of bed and said, *We've decided to send you to the awdy home.* I don't recall what we did; it might have been the time we burned our mother's new fur coat with matches, or maybe we wouldn't go to sleep. Whichever, my mother informed us that we couldn't take luggage and so had to wear all of the clothes we wanted to take with us. There were my brother and I, wearing several pants and shirts—and huge winter coats over that—standing at the doorway, little swaddled balls, our arms dangling almost straight out. My father on the phone: *Hello, awdy home? I've got two very bad boys here . . . I see, thank you.* He hung up. Well, he told my mother, *they're all full up tonight.* And then my mother to us: *Okay, you two. We can let you stay here tonight . . . but only if you promise to be good.*

I told this story at Thanksgiving about ten years ago, and my mother was mortified. *That never happened,* she said.

You made that up, my father said. *You make things up.*

No, I remember that, my brother said. *I remember; it was so dark out.*

I was thirteen and my brother was eleven when we went our separate ways; we had different friends and interests from then on. For the most part, different lives, no shared memories to speak of, or not.

———

At my wedding a couple of years ago, my brother, my best man, gave a toast. He talked about family and brotherhood and ended with a story: The two of us were on the same little-league team. He was second baseman, and I was catcher. During one game one time twenty-five years ago, a runner tried to steal second base. My brother recalled: *I can still see that throw. It was perfect. It fell right into my glove right in front of the base. We got the guy out.*

I don't remember it that way at all. What I remember to this day—sometimes while walking down the street and from out of nowhere—what I'll see: My little brother dashes to the base, crouches; the throw is low but he scoops it out of the dirt; he makes the perfect tag on the sliding runner; and then, dust. I can see it now.

the road to niamey

Thomas A. Kelley

It was the hot season in Niger, and my brother Michael and I were stuck in the village of Fandou-Berri, a cluster of grass huts next to a red dirt road that led nowhere. We were squatting under a millet-stalk lean-to hoping that a vehicle would pass and take us the seventy kilometers into the capital, Niamey. In our first few hours of waiting, Michael and I periodically shifted our positions under the lean-to to avoid the rays of sun that shone through the holes where desperately hungry goats and donkeys had ripped off stalks. But by mid-afternoon we sat still, resigned that our already-burnt skin would be scorched to a dull maroon.

In my Peace Corps days I sometimes would tire of waiting for a ride and walk the twenty kilometers to the nearest paved road. But four years had passed since I had left, and I had spent most of that time flat on my ass in law school classes. I wasn't sure I had the walk in me. And I was damned sure Michael didn't. For years he had been stronger and fitter than I, but he had ignored my advice to buy a broad-brim straw hat in Niamey, and instead had come out to the bush wearing his trusty old black cotton military-surplus hat. After two days in the blazing sun the black hat had fried his brains, and now he was staring blankly at the biscuit-colored dirt in front of him, puffing his pink cheeks in and out. Just breathing was an exertion. Every so often his tongue would pass over his lips and he'd begin to reach for a water bottle, but then pull his hand back when he remembered that we had only two liters left and might have to spend another night in the village.

We were not alone under the lean-to. A revolving delegation of village elders, most of them friends from the old days, sat with us staring at Michael and peppering me with questions and suggestions.

"Ifo no ni keyna ga te Americi ra?" ("What does your little brother do in America?")

"A ya loctoro locoliza no." ("He is studying to be a doctor.")

"Ni keyna, a ga ba wa ga'a gaabandi." ("Your little brother needs goat milk to strengthen him.")

"Ha a, nda ga'a han, a ga' a gunda dorandi." ("No, if he drinks milk it will make his stomach sick.")

I added the fact that Michael always got sick when he left the United States. The men laughed and Michael asked me what they were saying.

"I told them my little brother gets sick easily when he travels."

"Would you mind not referring to me as your little brother?"

"Birth order's important here. You're supposed to respect your older siblings."

I translated this exchange to the elders, and they agreed with me, nodding their heads vigorously.

Michael smiled and nodded back to them, then glared at me through swollen, mosquito-bitten eyes.

"Do you get pleasure out of this?" he asked.

I got up to stretch my legs and spotted a dust cloud a kilometer or so down the road.

"Michael, get your stuff ready."

As he arranged his bags, the elders rose slowly, murmuring customary Muslim exclamations and brushing dirt from their flowing robes, drifting in a bunch toward the center of the road. A truck rounded the bend a half kilometer from the village. A Toyota Land Cruiser pickup, an encouraging sign. Foreign-aid workers were the only ones who could afford such vehicles. I had never been passed in the bush by Europeans. We would be in Niamey for sunset cocktails at the Grand Hotel.

The truck did not slow as it headed up the hill. The driver, a bearded white man, began beeping the horn violently and flashing the headlights. By the time the elders realized that he did not intend to stop, it was too late for them to clear out of the way. The driver slammed on the brakes, sending red dirt flying and the dignified, robed men scrambling.

The driver was accelerating away when he spotted my brother and me standing in front of the lean-to. He again slammed on the brakes. He leaned across the passenger, a white woman, and screamed out the window, "Etes vous médecins?" I told him no, but my brother was a medical student. He threw open his door, vaulted onto the road and ran around to where we were standing, motioning for us to look at something in the back. I could see an old man sitting on a tire and an old woman—his wife I assumed—crouching next to him, holding a bundle in her arms. But the Frenchman stood at the side of the truck bed and pointed to its floor, saying, "Venez ici. Regardez cette femme."

A young woman was lying at the feet of the older couple. She was barely conscious and curled up in the fetal position. She was wrapped in colorful African cloths and a thick, gray blanket. Blood had soaked through to mix with sand and grime and pool in the dents and between the ridges of the metal floor of the pickup. She had just given birth and was hemorrhaging. The bundle in the old woman's arms was a baby, her grandchild.

The Frenchman asked if there was anything Michael could do for the young woman. I told him there was a rural health clinic in Hamdallaye, less than thirty kilometers away. I thought we should try to get her there as quickly as possible. Michael said that it would make sense for him to locate the source of the bleeding and assess the severity of the situation.

"Michael, I'm concerned about the implications of your taking responsibility for this woman's care."

I said this in the cool voice I'd practiced for emotionally overwrought clients, but even as I spoke the words sounded ridiculous, wooden. I'm not sure what I was thinking. Maybe it was a legitimate worry that we should not interfere in these people's lives. Maybe I had become a thoroughly indoctrinated lawyer in the four years since leaving Africa. Maybe it was the simple fact that I had been bossing Michael around for twenty-six years, that I wasn't willing to see him suddenly take control.

He stared at me, puzzled, knitting his eyebrows and cocking his head slightly. The young woman moaned. The Frenchman looked at me anxiously. When I turned again toward Michael he was already climbing into the back of the truck. The Frenchman and I ran around toward the driver's side and I yelled back to Michael, "You're not a doctor." We roared off, spitting dirt at the chattering cluster of village elders.

———

At the clinic, we wrapped the woman in a woven-grass prayer mat that had been sitting on the dirt in the village square and carried her into the examining room. There was no table or stretcher, so we put her on the floor. Without the truck's wind, flies swarmed around the blood that seeped from her wraps. The two nurses on duty came in from a back room and walked around the woman in circles. They were speaking a language I did not understand, but they seemed to be debating whether or not to touch her. Finally, one of them squatted down in front of her and began pushing her wraps up so he could look between her legs. Blood was pouring out in a slow, even flow. The squatting nurse stood bolt upright. The other nurse backed away. "Il n'y a rien qu' on peut faire," one of them said. He told us that if we still wanted to help, we could take her to the hospital in Niamey. There were doctors there, he said.

My brother had drifted across the examining room and taken up a post staring out the open window toward the town square. I walked over and stood behind him.

"We need to get her back into the truck," I said.

He turned around. He looked like he was going to cry. His eyes were red-rimmed, the color exaggerated because of the pale dust covering his face. His teeth were clenched as if he were holding back a scream. I could see his jaw muscles twitching. It was an unfamiliar sight. I had not seen him cry since I had split his chin playing football when he was eight and I was twelve. As adults we had been together through funerals, family alcohol interventions, and our parents' divorce. I'd always been the crier. More than once my brother had seen me bawl and sob myself into exhaustion. But I had not seen him shed so much as a single tear.

I knew what he was thinking. We had grown up watching my father and grandfather, both doctors, jump right in whenever anyone was sick or hurt. As children we heard many times about the day my grandfather had saved the life of his fourth son, also named Michael, who had been hit by a car. Our grandfather had rushed his unconscious son into the basement, gone to the tool box, grabbed a hand auger, and drilled holes in the boy's skull to relieve the pressure on his brain. The child kept passing out and my grandfather kept drilling holes. When I was sixteen and learning to drive, my brother, father, and grandfather were in the car with me when we came across an auto accident in which several people had been hurt. One woman was wandering around stunned and bleeding and another was lying semi-conscious on the ground. The police were just arriving. I slowed the car and was inching by the wreck when my father and grandfather simultaneously opened their doors and leapt out. They hadn't discussed it. I don't think they had even looked at each other. They went to work examining the victims and then giving instructions to the arriving paramedics.

This was, I knew, one of the only things my brother found to admire in the men from whom we were descended. Their ability to act decisively, to be of use in a crisis. Somehow my brother's love and bitterness toward our father converged in Michael's desire to be a doctor.

I knew this, yet as I stood there trying to think of something to say, what came out of my mouth was, "You're not a doctor yet."

"I know I can help," Michael said.

"This is not your country."

We wrapped the woman back up in the grass mat and carried her across the dirt yard of the clinic to the waiting pickup truck.

Dusk is an hour of gentle beauty in West Africa, and when we reached Niamey the chaos of the traffic-clogged dirt streets and the brutal heat of the day had given way to the soft orange glow of fading light passing through the dust of the streets and the smoke from evening cooking fires. As we raced past the Petit Marché on the way to the hospital, the beggars, beginning their evening prayer ablutions, paused to extend hands of solicitation. We drove down a dirt path to the hospital's emergency entrance. The courtyard was bustling with patients' families delivering evening meals. Women dressed in traditional panyas carried metal pots stacked on their heads. They slowed to watch the strange spectacle of a Frenchman running into the dark emergency reception area while two Americans delivered a limp, bleeding *nigerienne*.

By the time Michael and I arrived on the terrace outside the emergency room, professionals in white coats had arrived, pushing a gurney. I noticed that it was covered with a clean sheet. We hefted the woman onto the mattress and the doctors wheeled her into the dark caverns of the hospital. Her parents paused to thank us, then turned to follow the trail of blood.

I followed Michael back to the truck. The Frenchman and his wife were already there, sitting on the tailgate smoking cigarettes. I leaned against the side to catch my breath and watch the people stream in and out of the hospital. Out of the corner of my eye I could see Michael rummaging through our bags. I tried to think of something to say.

"You did the right thing. We got her to a hospital, to doctors. She's going to be all right." I said it without conviction and it was clear that he didn't believe me. He was shaking his head and avoiding my eyes as he opened and closed zippers on his pack.

He found what he was looking for: our remaining bottles of water. He opened one and began rinsing his hands. He was bending over at the waist, keeping the water close to the ground so it wouldn't splatter dirt on his feet. I asked him not to waste the water. It was expensive and I was thirsty.

He looked up at me and I saw that he was crying. This time there were tears streaming down his cheeks. "I'm covered in blood, you fucking idiot."

He was. There was blood all over his hands and arms, some dried, some fresh. There were large splotches on his T-shirt and pants.

At the mention of blood, it occurred to me that I had unconsciously been rubbing my toes together, trying to get rid of something sticky. I looked down at my flip-flops and tried to pick out the details in the fading light. I had been wearing flip-flops since our arrival in the country, and my feet were pocked with bug bites and blisters and sores. The whole mess was covered with blood. It was not until that moment that the problem dawned on me. Surely it was okay, I reasoned. She was a bush woman and HIV was concentrated in the cities.

As I considered this, staring at my feet as if they belonged to someone else, I realized that my brother was saying something.

"Wash your goddamn feet," he repeated.

I didn't respond.

Then he was on his knees in front of me, pouring the water, carefully rubbing one of the largest sores with his thumb, washing the blood away.

you can't kill the rooster

David Sedaris

When I was young, my father was transferred and our family moved from western New York state to Raleigh, North Carolina. IBM had relocated a great many northerners and, together, we made relentless fun of our new neighbors and their poky, backward way of life. Rumors circulated that natives ran stills out of their tool sheds and referred to their house cats as "good eatin'." Our parents coached us to never use the titles "ma'am" or "sir" when speaking to a teacher or shopkeeper. Tobacco was acceptable in the form of a cigarette, but should any of us experiment with plug or snuff, we would be automatically disinherited. Mountain Dew was forbidden and our speech was monitored for the slightest hint of a Raleigh accent. Use the phrase "y'all" and, before you knew it, you'd find yourself in a haystack french-kissing an underage goat. Along with grits and hush puppies, the abbreviated form of "you all" was a dangerous step on an insidious path leading straight to the doors of the Baptist Church.

We might not have been the wealthiest people in town, but at least we weren't one of them.

Portfolio I

His Holiness the Dalai Lama, 62; Tendzin Choegyal, 51, adviser

Eight years before Tendzin Choegyal was born, a search party of Tibetan monks identified three-year-old Lhamo Dhondup as the fourteenth incarnation of the Dalai Lama. "There was never a time that His Holiness was only a brother to me," Choegyal said recently. "I had to share him with a nation, with a world. Yet at the same time, he was also a very loving and protective brother. He was always looking out for me."

Photographed by Stephane Sednaoui at the Dalai Lama's Residence in Exile in Dharamsala, India, March 18, 1998.

Martin Scorsese, 55, filmmaker; Frank Scorsese, 62, printer

"Let me put it this way. The films I make are not about my brother and myself, but it comes from a brothers' relationship, a blood relationship, and a responsibility to each other and the family. It's all there in the movies—a little bit in *Goodfellas* but primarily in *Raging Bull* and *Mean Streets*. There are lots of feelings that maybe I wasn't able to verbalize that came out in the pictures." —**Martin Scorsese**

Photographed by Marc Hom at the Cappa Productions Screening Room in New York City, March 17, 1998.

Albert Brooks, 50, actor, writer, director; Super Dave Osborne, ageless daredevil; Cliff Einstein, 59, advertising executive

"We are very close. And that's kind of the text, with no subtext. We just really do like each other."

—Cliff Einstein

Photographed by Dan Winters in Hollywood, February 28, 1998.

The Heath brothers, jazz greats: Jimmy Heath, 72; Albert "Tootie" Heath, 63; Percy Heath, 75

"All of us learned a little bit from how Percy moves though the world. Percy sees the world through a European perspective. He loves Europe, he loves the lifestyle, fine wine, European food, France, Italy. Jimmy is more of a New Yorker, New York is it for him. He doesn't care much for the fine foods and wine. I'm more Afrocentric, Africa is the central source of my inspiration. My instrument led me into that, took me away from the total jazz idiom, makes me look at other cultures differently." —Albert "Tootie" Heath

Photographed by Larry Fink at SoHo Studios in New York City, December 23, 1998.

James Garner, 70, actor; Jack Garner, 71, golf pro

"We're closer now than we probably were in the middle part of our lives. I always admired Jack and envied him—he's a great athlete. He was a quarterback, a star basketball player, he played professional baseball for twelve years, and then he turned pro golfer. I was always in his footsteps, and I was never quite that good. And he's much more outgoing than I am. Until I know you, I'm shy, but Jack knows everybody right off the bat." —**James Garner**

Photographed by Harry Benson at the Peninsula Hotel in Beverly Hills, March 2, 1998.

Jesse Louis Jackson Jr., 33, congressman; Yusef DuBois Jackson, 28, business executive and attorney;
Jonathan Jackson, 33, real estate developer

"It was exciting growing up in our home. One of the many things we enjoyed doing was answering the telephone. We could always take a minute or two with people like Percy Sutton, Sammy Davis Jr., Reverend Samuel Proctor, or the White House, before we'd say 'Dad, telephone.' As we grew older we realized this was a little out of the ordinary." —**Jesse Jackson Jr.**

Photographed by Michael Lavine in Chicago, Illinois, March 15, 1999

Bobby Farrelly, 40, filmmaker;
Peter Farrelly, 41, filmmaker;
chicken, age unknown, egg-layer
Photographed by Michael Grecco
in Los Angeles, January 7, 1999.

Norman Marbury, 27, special-education teacher; Zach Marbury, 18, student athlete; Stephon Marbury, 21, professional basketball player; Eric Marbury, 38, construction worker; Donald Marbury, 34, gym teacher

Photographed by Edward Gajdel in Suitland, Maryland, November 26, 1998.

rules of the house

Richard Ford

I wish there had been a moment in my young life, twenty-three years ago, when I could've thought to myself, "What I think I'll do now is join a college fraternity." Because if so, there might've been a moment when I could as easily have said, "No, I believe I won't join a college fraternity. I'm not that kind of fellow."

What I did back then was not give either possibility a thought. I simply joined. Pledged. Sigma Chi. Tom Selleck and Dave Letterman's bunch—the famous one with the sentimental song and the pretty sweetheart who later becomes your wife.

For a certain kind of boy at a certain tender age, fraternity is simply a given. A go-along guy, who wants friends. A guy with standards he can't understand. For this kind of boy conformity is a godsend. And I was that kind of boy.

In the long run, of course, fraternities have more or less the ethical dimension of a new hairstyle or a soft-drink flavor or a dance step you learn to perfection, then forget about entirely. And I don't feel particularly sorry to have been a member, since I'm suspicious of revising my past, and dislike the idea that anything I did and can remember so vividly was completely worthless. But still, I would like to have *chosen* to join, to have back those "decisions" I made by not deciding. Nothing, after all, is as venerable as nervy volition exerted in early age.

Like all conformists, we did not think of ourselves as conformists. We were men. Individuals and individualists. We knew what we knew. We prized life's lonelier roads, we were hard guys to convince of things. Stiletto-eyed, serious, even grave. The fraternity meant to solidify these things and add some others—"fairness, decency, good manners." We winked, nodded, nested chins in our palms when listening, wrinkled our brows, clinched Winstons in our teeth, dealt a fair hand. We meant something, and we knew it.

Yet we also knew how to let down the gates for a good time when the right times came. We knew how to treat a woman. How to confide. We were easy in the company of men. We knew where to draw the line. Imagine our surprise, then, at finding an entire group of other guys who felt as we did about practically everything.

Independents, those sallow fellows who did not join fraternities, who stayed in the dorm and sculled around the shallows of organized social life—blazerless—suffered, we felt, the mark of undesirability and championed a mean, cast-out status. Loneliness, unprotectedness were features of that bad idea. Independence did not have the novelty it would come to have. Then, it only meant left out, which it does still. And none of us had stomachs for that.

Our bunch had standards, but to be initiated to Sigma Chi, Michigan State, 1963, you were still required to pick up a stuffed olive off the chapter-room floor using nothing but the naked cheeks of your behind; and, while many "actives" watched and cheered, deliver the olive to a small, waiting Dixie cup. You still had to sit six hours straight on the hard edge of a hard chair, knees together, blindfolded, while somebody played Ravel's *Bolero*, fortissimo, directly into your ears. You had to do many, many painful push-ups. You had to let the older boys scream obscenities and insults in your face, blow cigar smoke in your eyes, and breathe on you until they were tired of it. You had to tramp out into the frozen Michigan night in search of nothing less than a white cross—the fraternity's sacred emblem—which, of course, wasn't there. You had to bray like a donkey, buzz like a fly, bleat like a goat, be scorned, scourged, ridiculed, and insulted until they let you join them. It must've seemed like a good idea.

Exacting decisions had already been made about the people who *weren't* being initiated. We were, after all, chiefly in the excluding business. This guy had "the breath of death"; this guy had "bad choppers." This guy has "the handshake of a fish." We didn't want Jews, blacks, Orientals, gays, women, big fatties, or cripples. Yo-Yo Ma couldn't have been a Sigma Chi. Neither could Steven Spielberg or Justice Marshall.

We *did* want "face men," jocks, wild guys, rich guys, guys with class, guys with sisters, guys with "nice threads," "real characters," guys willing to make fools of themselves and others. Guys who didn't think this was all bullshit. Good guys, in other words.

I've never seen the movie *Animal House*. But from the previews I've concluded Sigma Chi, in my day, was a lot like that, more or less. We called ourselves by animal names—the Pigeon, the Pig, the Guppie, the Armadillo, the Whale (there were also vegetables—the Eggplant, the Rutabaga, the Tomato, the Carrot, the Root). We put people's heads in toilets. We lighted our farts. We dropped our trousers in public. We drank and pissed on things. We danced. We shouted. We groped. We gave the finger. We got sick. We wore coats and ties. We were men and knew no bottom line.

A good question to ask of all this, I suppose, is: "Were we friends, all of us?" And the answer would have to be—not that much, if friendships are things meant to last a long time. I remember detesting some of my brothers, mocking others, lying to them, pitying them, bird-dogging *their* sweethearts. One boy, now a veterinarian, I sucker-punched at a party, reshaping one of his nostrils forever—I forget precisely why. By the time I'd been in a year, I was already certain I did not belong (though neither did I want out), so that I became, for a while, aloof with superiority. These guys were just children, Gothics to be brought along for amusement, on earth for me to observe. This, I think, is also what conformists do.

What I learned from being a Sigma Chi, though, is enough to make me not regret it. I learned that an experience need not be ennobling or noble for good to come out of it. This, after all, is the alma mater of comedy. I learned that even from a brotherhood one could get free, as some did, though it wasn't easy. There was red tape. Soul-searching. Hard feelings. You needed to renounce more than a moment, a scene, a situation. I learned, in fact, that life itself could be thought of as just a series of alliances entered into for a time and a goal, and abandonable without prejudice. All this, I think, is instructive of the value of institutions both good and bad.

I also learned that buffoonery, prejudice, treachery, resentment, pettiness—all the poorer instincts—can often go hand in glove with demonstrations of friendship and companionability, and that those impulses are not necessarily even alien, but are merely humors within the larger human dramaturgy. We must decide which humor will dominate. Many times, in those days, I asked myself, "Can I do this, think this, say this, and still be your brother?" And the answer was almost always *yes*.

Is all this then, I wonder, what the fraternity meant us to learn? Is this what the grip meant? The secrets? *In hoc signo vinces?* Maybe. But I doubt it. It had something else in mind, I think. Something nobler sounding, but that in a complex, importance-seeking world, wouldn't work; that would turn us into Babbitts and, later, Meursaults. We were phonies, poseurs, bores, joke-masters, stupids, preposterous boys who wore our importance like uniforms but signified nothing—me not the least of them. And in truth if I learned anything at all, it might've been that I did not have to stay exactly that way forever.

half done

Scott Raab

The house was small—a rancher, basementless, a GI Bill, Levittown-era piece of plywood crap—with tiny rooms. However small I was, the rooms were much smaller than I needed them to be, especially the bedroom Dave and I shared. I was never alone, always crowded. Small, helpless, and crowded.

I wanted to be alone, just left alone. *Leave me alone*: I must have spoken that phrase ten thousand times as a child. Or if not alone, alone with my mom and dad. I must have known the taste of alone, either way, because I was firstborn. David didn't come along until I was two-and-a-half. Then he was always there, even smaller and more helpless, but, by dint of his existence, crowding me, supplanting me, usurping my place. I have no memory of life without him there, no memory of life alone.

If there ever was a time I was not mad at him, I don't recall that, either. My fury boiled over as far back as memory. He had an Emmett Kelly doll, and that small, sad clown's face drove me wild. I tore it apart. I can still feel the cotton wadding in my hands as I ripped its arms and legs from their sockets. I don't know what made me snap; I snapped, that's all. I don't remember David's reaction, or being punished for it or lying about it or feeling a moment's regret. I just remember the dark circles beneath Emmett Kelly's eyes, the burning inside me, the tufts of cotton like gone flesh clenched in my small hands.

There was no aftermath, or maybe there was only aftermath, a sense that rage might have no boundaries, might be acted upon without consequence, even if the object of that rage were flesh and blood, even my own flesh and blood.

I tore that clown doll limb from limb, and still Dave was there. Then Robert was born. That I truly wanted to be left alone had become the mootest of points. I could have torn David limb from limb, and the job would've been only half done.

"Only half done": This seems somehow funny to me now, both amusing and ironic. Ironic because, although its locus has shifted—I treasure my brothers—I still burn with that same rage when I feel crowded by life, when I feel helpless and small. It stuffs my lungs, boils over in my brain. I hear it choking my voice. I want to cry, but I can't, can't cry, can't even speak without a tremor in my voice. I want to tear someone limb from limb—my wife, my boss, my neighbor—want to rip them apart so they'll leave me the fuck alone, but my hands are trembling too hard to hold a pen.

Ha ha. Leave me alone. Leave me alone to be consumed by my rage.

My hands did not tremble when they were small: They went to work.

We left the small rancher behind for the Golden State, left the suburbs of Cleveland for the San Fernando Valley back when the valley was still mostly farms and ranches, back when Route 66 was the western trail. I rode out there on 66 with my old man; my mother flew with my brothers to meet us. I remember clearly and with pleasure the wonder of that trip, alone with my father. Not the Meramec caverns or the bison in Oklahoma, not the moonrise in Albuquerque or the Petrified Forest: No, what I remember in my bones is my father's grown-man smell and the sound of his voice.

He was not small. He was not helpless. And I did not feel small and helpless with him.

This house was a little bigger, but guess who was there, in my room and in my face. But I liked my new school and I liked girls, in a third-grade sort of way. The weather was good and I spent a lot of time outside. I lost track of David for a while, lost track of my rage.

We had been in California a couple of years when I came home from school one day to find David waiting for me in front of the house. He was crying. He told me that we were moving back to Cleveland without our father. This turned out to be true: our folks were getting a divorce, and there was nothing to be done about it. My mother—this was 1962, when divorce was a serious taint and divorcées rarely had career prospects—moved back to Cleveland and into her parents' house with her three sons.

I don't know which of us felt most crowded and helpless then—me, my mother, my brothers, or my grandfather, who could not have expected to spend his retirement years in a three-bedroom, one-bathroom house with his wife, his grown daughter, and three young boys—but I know whose rage got big, bigger every day.

I had well-meaning people telling me that I was the man of the house now, that I had to be a helpmate to my mother and a father to my brothers. I was ten years old and hurting; this advice did not sit well with me. I missed my father deeply.

Now the three of us—Bob, Dave, and I—all shared one bedroom. There were no boundaries anymore.

I did not like living with my grandparents; I didn't like my new school. I was getting fatter every day—so was Dave—and the girls made fun of me. I couldn't lose track of him or contain the fury inside of me. Some of it went into poems and stories, and still does; some of it came out when I listened to rock and roll, and still does. But the vast, ugly bulk of it I visited on David, verbally and physically. I told him to shut up whenever he spoke to me. When he wouldn't, which was most of the time, I would punch him as hard as I could until he did. I was getting stronger and more angry every day.

One afternoon I jerked David over an ottoman, just grabbed him by the arm and yanked. Something tore or cracked; our mother took him to the hospital, and he came home wearing a cast. I'm certain that my mother screamed at me, but she screamed at us all the time, every day, about everything. The cast gave me no remorse. I don't remember Dave's face when I hurt him. He didn't cry. Whatever rage he felt, he contained, too small and helpless to do much about it.

Not long after that, I broke Bob's arm. He was small and quick, and I was chasing after him, with a pillow, of all things. I beat on Bob less frequently, but my temper was growing. What pissed me off was that I had been bending over for something, and Bob gave me a shove from behind. For this I chased him, and when I got close enough, I hauled off and swung the pillow as hard as I could at his trailing arm. The doctor told my mother that it took two hundred pounds of thrust to break his wrist; at least that's what she screamed at me.

They hurt, they healed; I didn't care. I don't know how to explain that, except to say that these were my brothers. They seemed not to hold the pain I caused them against me, not then and not now. We loved each other—we were all we had, is how it felt—and if not for my rage and their subsequent pain, that love had no voice. Besides, no one else laid a hand on them. That I wouldn't allow. They were mine.

One summer David and I were sent to California for a stay with our father. He sized up the situation pretty quickly and sent Dave to karate lessons. At least that's what I was told: I saw no evidence, no kicks, no chops. The truth is that David was not then and not ever a shrinking violet. He stood up and took his licks; if he never picked a fight with me, that's because he never had to. In California that summer, we went at it hard one afternoon, trading blows until we were both crying, still throwing punches. It wasn't the pain, and there was no rage left after a while, just two fat boys belting each other with tears running down their cheeks. No one else was home.

"You're the snot from my nose," I'd tell him. "You're the shit from my ass."

I taunted him about everything, including the karate lessons. I didn't tell him he was my brother, and that I loved him.

———

I don't remember where I got the boxing gloves. Certainly I didn't buy them: I had no money. Fired from McDonald's, I had no job. I stole my cigarettes from my mother. I was in the tenth grade then, sullen, lonely, mean, interested in neither school—most days I didn't bother to go—nor girls.

We were out of our grandparents' house and back in the tiny rancher, which had been rented out all those years. Our mother, a school secretary now, was still screaming; our father still lived in California. I had one of the tiny bedrooms to myself; Dave and Bob shared the other. I still felt crowded and helpless. But not small: I was big. I mean big. I went well over two–fifty and I was strong as a horse.

We were in the living room, the three of us brothers. Dave and I laced up the gloves. Did he have a choice? Did I?

It was, no doubt, the purest punch I ever threw, so sweetly perfect that I felt no jolt, nothing at all, when it met skin and skull. It was a right cross straight from the shoulder that traveled no more than six inches before it met David's head just above his left ear. His eyes went round and wide, then closed. He crashed into the orange lamp sitting on the coffee table on his way to the carpet.

He woke up after a minute, maybe less. That's the last time I remember hitting him. I didn't feel shame or regret. It scared me, a little. I hadn't been angry, not especially—and that scared me, not David going black and hitting the floor. Rage was all there was of me.

I don't know how we got over it; I don't know if we ever have, or whether there really was anything to get over. We were, after all, brothers, and that's not something you get over or put behind you. I went away to college—not far enough, but away, out of the tiny house. I got into plenty of fights, but not with my brothers.

Dave went away to college, a different school. We've rarely lived in the same town since, but we talk often and there's nothing we don't talk about, including old times. One day, years later, we were both in Cleveland, back at my mother's tiny house for a meal. Bob was there, too. Dave was in the kitchen, carving the meat; the rest of us were sitting around the dining room table.

There was pounding on the counter by the sink, and I saw David had water pouring out of his mouth. His face was scarlet. He had popped a slice of beef into his mouth and he was choking. I went into the kitchen, grabbed him from behind around the belly, and jerked up hard. Out flew the meat.

"Thanks a lot," David said when he caught his breath.

Later, outside the house, I told him that I hoped I'd made up for some of the shit behind us. He laughed. I laughed. What else is there to do? The same blood beats in our hearts.

———

The Nuzum brothers
top row: Abraham, 7; Simon, 8; Timothy, 10; John, 13
second row: Noah, 6; Jeremiah, 11; Willie, 9; Daniel, 23
third row: Tony, 23; Alex, 9, Joshua, 8; David, 6, Zachariah, 3
front row: Samuel, 5; Charlie, 10; Jake, 8; Michael, 7

Shuttling around Holland, Ohio, in a big yellow school bus, or working out together at their own martial arts center downtown, the Nuzum family is hard to miss. Joanne and Scott Nuzum have raised thirty children (twenty-one boys and nine girls), twenty-nine of whom they've adopted. "Many of the kids are brothers and sisters who had been separated in different foster homes—so in some ways, the agencies couldn't keep them together," says Mrs. Nuzum. "We got to put them back together."

Many of the Nuzum brothers are "special needs" children, affected by varying degrees of mental retardation, autism, cerebral palsy, or emotional disabilities. Because of the separation of siblings and the constant visits to doctors and therapists, many of them never knew the true meaning of family. "We've been able to provide some security, so they can be kids if they want to," says Mrs. Nuzum. "We try to teach the kids not just the love part, but teamwork and responsibility. They know how to feed, how to diaper, they know how to care. A lot of them didn't know how to care. They were selfish, but they had to be selfish in order to survive."

Danny Nuzum, the oldest sibling and the only birth child, has been a mainstay of affection for the whole family. Now a tai-kwon-do instructor at the Nuzums' martial arts center, he acts as a big brother for all his siblings. "He's accepted everyone from the beginning," says Joanne. "He tells everyone he's the oddball."

Photographed by Andrea Modica at Nuzum's Health & Martial Arts Club in Holland, Ohio, January 3, 1999.

the co-zygotes almanac

Random Entries from Forty Years of Twin Brotherhood

Steve and Mark O'Donnell

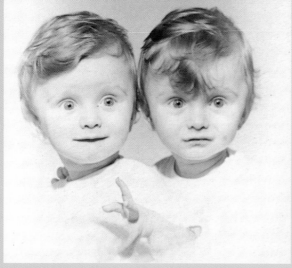

CHRISTIAN NAMES OF O'DONNELL TWINS

- Stephen Michael
- Mark Patrick

PARENTS

- Mother: American-born daughter of Slovenian immigrants who, throughout life, resented having to pay for the bananas they were handed at Ellis Island, figuring they were a "welcome gift."
- Father: American-born son of Irish immigrants who, throughout life, claimed descent from "kings" of Donegal.

NUMBER OF IRISHMEN NOT DESCENDED FROM "KINGS"

Zero.

BIRTHPLACE AND IRRELEVANT INTERESTING DETAIL

Cleveland, Ohio, where through the 1960s the public library displayed a book bound in human flesh and a jar of 3,000-year-old raisins from what is now Iraq.

YEAR OF TWINS' BIRTH AS SIGNIFICANT IN CLEVELAND HISTORY

After setting American League record for victories, Indians go to '54 World Series against the New York Giants, which they lose, due in part to an amazing catch by Willie Mays. Do not return to World Series for forty years, when they lose again.

"AGE" DIFFERENCE BETWEEN TWIN BROTHERS (AS DEFINED BY ARRIVAL IN REGULAR ATMOSPHERE)

Five minutes.

FERTILITY DRUGS TAKEN BY MOTHER
Beyond the Holy Eucharist, none.

ONE THEORY AS TO WHY TWINS ARRIVED AFTER NINE OTHER INDIVIDUAL BIRTHS
The family ate a lot of day-old bread.

ANOTHER THEORY
Reproductive system getting wacky under strains of mass production, like old cereal machine starting to spew out figure-eight Cheerios.

HOW WELDER DAD WAS ADDRESSED BY NURSE AT HOSPITAL WHERE WIFE HAD DELIVERED ELEVEN BABIES
"Good morning, Doctor."

INDICATION THAT AMERICAN BIRTHING PROCESS STILL HAD A GRAB-BAG SPONTANEITY TO IT AT MID-CENTURY
Delivery room staff unaware there were two babies until Steve, the firstborn, was already out.

NOTEWORTHY DIFFERENCE IN TWINS AT AGE ZERO
• Steve: three pounds six ounces.
• Mark: three pounds four ounces.
Steve dogged throughout life by accusation of "hogging the placenta."

AT AGE FIVE
• Steve: right-handed.
• Mark: left-handed.

AT AGE SEVEN
• Steve draws exploding Messerschmitts.
• Mark draws giraffes wearing clothes.

AT AGE TEN
• Steve prefers Almond Joy bar.
• Mark, Mounds.

AT AGE FIFTEEN
• Steve prefers Flatt & Scruggs.
• Mark, Rodgers & Hammerstein.

AT AGE TWENTY
• Steve prefers sex with women.
• Mark, men.
(Role of Mounds bar remains undetermined.)

AT AGE THIRTY
• Steve believes it's better to shave after you shower.
• Mark, before.
(Not really as interesting as the sex thing.)

ONE THEORY EXPLAINING HOW SUPERFICIAL DUPLICATES CAN HAVE DIFFERENT SEXUAL ORIENTATIONS
It all has to do with your environment.

ANOTHER THEORY
It has nothing to do with your environment.

ULTIMATE PRIMACY OF NATURE OR NURTURE
Yeah, like we're gonna settle that here.

Other Opposite Traits in O'Donnell Twins, More Easily Explainable

• Hair naturally parts on different sides.
• Amblyopia, or "Lazy Eye," in opposite eyes. Wore eye patches on opposite sides (not cool pirate style but a wan flesh-tone).
• Whorls of hair spiral out in clockwise and counter-clockwise directions, like water down the drain above and below the equator.

Physical "Oppositeness" as a Common Phenomenon

"Mirror image" effect consistent with the norm for identical twins. Like peeling silly putty off a comic strip, only with DNA. Though the hearts are both on the left side, which kind of throws doubt on the whole thing, doesn't it?

Unpleasant Detail About Physical Similarities

Blemishes eerily appeared in same parts of teen twins' faces.

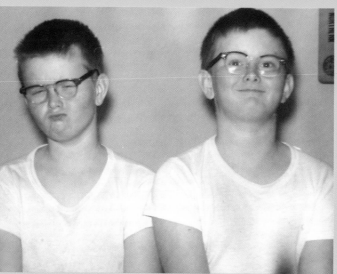

Frequently Heard Childhood Taunts

"Ike and Mike! They look alike!"
"Am I seein' double?"
"It's Pete and Repeat!"
"Are you you or are you your brother?"
"Which one of you is smarter?"

Which One of the Twins Actually is Smarter?

According to the authorities, Mark. But the authorities also insist hot tea quenches your thirst better than iced tea, and *come on*!

Bizarre Mnemonic Device Having to Do with Chins

Uncertain grade school teachers lift twins' chins, looking for crescent-shaped gash left by fall onto bare metal bike handlebar; coo "S for scar and S for Stephen."

Class-Switching Activity

Routinely engaged in at pre-collegiate level. Less as wacky hi-jinx than practical way to get extra study halls when needed. Noteworthy only as most-asked question about "fun" of being twins by non-twins.

Example of Above (Non-Practical)

Some degree of "fun" experienced switching marching-band positions and instruments with negligible detriment to sounds of Sousa. (Character correlations may be cautiously drawn to instruments involved: baritone horn and flute.)

Actual Illegal Chicanery That Twins Can't Be Touched For, Now

Mark takes three-hour-long math test for Steve that has a proctor checking photo IDs at the door.

Trendy Word That Applies to Recognition That Mark, The Left-Handed Homosexual

BROTHER, IS BETTER AT MATH THAN HIS RIGHT-
HANDED HETEROSEXUAL TWIN (VIS-À-VIS MATH
AS A "LEFT-BRAIN" FUNCTION)
Counter-intuitive.

REVERSE STEREOTYPE APPLICABLE TO NON-GAY TWIN
Fussier housekeeper of the two.

HOW A NINTH-GRADE BIOLOGY TEACHER WAS
STUNNED:
Mr. Bell, explaining the influence of environment,
asserts "No two organisms are exactly alike. Not even
Mark and Steve here." A mutual sense of vaudeville
timing causes the twins to respond instantly in chip-
per unison, *"You're absolutely right, Mr. Bell."*

MILD EXAMPLE OF VAUNTED TELEPATHY
Ongoing pointlessness of participating in parlor
games together. One twin rises from couch. As first
gesture begins, other flatly states, "A Perfect Day for
Bananafish." Non-twin players, suspicious and angry,
consider appealing to the Charades Commissioner.

STRONGER EXAMPLE OF VAUNTED TELEPATHY
While seniors in high school, Steve spends night at
friend's house, where group gets stoned. About midnight, Steve, the least-stoned, drives car to pick up
pizza, singing "The Mighty Quinn" with buddy Bob,
who's riding shotgun. Steve pantomimes Three Stooge
move of pulling off steering wheel and handing it to
Bob. Next morning, Steve returns to family home.
Before any conversation takes place, Mark describes
dream he had some time between eleven and two of
Steve driving car, with music all around, goofily
pulling off steering wheel and handing it to person
next to him. *Brrrr.*

DEGREE OF INSIGHT PROVIDED BY VAUNTED
TELEPATHY INTO EACH OTHER'S SEXUAL
ORIENTATION
Less than you'd think.

ADJECTIVE THIS ANOMALY BRINGS TO MIND
Mysterious.

RELATIONSHIP OF TWINS TO OLDER BROTHERS
(SPORTS METAPHOR)
Three older brothers, Denny, Tony, and Bill, all ath-
letes and future engineers, accept frivolous twins as
ornamental mascots in slightly embarrassing cos-
tumes doing clumsy cartwheels on sidelines while real
achievements take place out on the gridiron.

RELATIONSHIP OF TWINS TO OLDER BROTHERS (SCIENCE FICTION METAPHOR)

Twins as freakish ambassadors from a silly planet on goodwill mission to the mining asteroid.

ROLE OF "OLDER" TWIN (DIPLOMATIC METAPHOR CONTINUED)

The Sibling Switzerland. Go-between for big brothers and younger twin and vice versa. Transitional figure between pure oddity and apparent normality.

TALENTS OF OLDER BROTHERS NOT EVINCED BY TWINS

• Woodworking
• Joining metals
• Handball
• Engine repair
• Perfect spiral passes
• Getting through Navy boot camp and into Submarine Service
• Mechanical drawing
• Fisticuffs
• Two-fingered, high-decibel whistling

TALENTS OF TWINS NOT EVINCED BY OLDER BROTHERS

• Construction of shoe-box dioramas depicting tea party in Wonderland or bloody Omaha Beach
• Mimicry of foreign accents (i.e., Moronic Swede)

WELDER DAD'S STANDARD PREFACE TO RESTRAINED EXPRESSION OF ANNOYANCE WITH TWIN SONS

"You boys might be smart about *some* things . . ."

SMALL PERK ENJOYED BY WELDER DAD DUE TO LIMITED SMARTNESS OF TWIN SONS

In promotion that lasted for years, six pairs of Indians tickets sent back if you mailed in a straight-A report card.

SHOCKING DISCOVERY ABOUT "STRAIGHT-A" TICKETS DEAL

Indians ticket office would send six pairs of tickets even if the report card you sent in had C's and D's all over it.

WHOLESOME WAYS STRAIGHT-ARROW OLDER BROTHERS SHOWED LOVE AND CONCERN FOR KID-BROTHER TWINS

Served as mentors in fishing, ice-skating, and model making, as well as bulwark against predatory punks in pointy shoes and Banlon shirts from up the block. Repeatedly fixed bicycle gears, which twins seem baffled by. Hauled twins' asses out of situations where they were floundering in deep water, stranded in trees, or close to catching fire.

EXAMPLE OF PAINFUL BUT PLAYFUL INTERACTION

Older brothers' regular administration of stinging "Dutch Rubs" (a.k.a. Electro-noogies) to twins' scalps, rarely commenting on natural wonder of clockwise and counter-clockwise whorls.

JUST PLAIN PAINFUL INTERACTION WITH OLDER BROTHERS

When movie *Land of the Pharaohs* starring Jack Hawkins came on TV, an older brother chirps "Land of the Fairies—starring Mark O'Donnell!"

LIKELIHOOD OLDER BROTHERS ACTUALLY IMAGINED MARK WOULD GROW UP GAY

Slight.

ARMCHAIR PSYCHOLOGIST'S PROBABLE PONTIFICATIONS ON IMPORTANCE OF BIRTH ORDER TO PERSONALITY OF "YOUNGER" TWIN

With twins as last of ten children, Mark, the younger of pair, is at absolute bottom of household pecking order and likelier to retreat into a fanciful interior life (i.e., filling three spiral notebooks with a musical comedy based on his pet toads, including the show-stopping "Tadpoles Are Bustin' Out All Over").

FRATERNAL CATCHPHRASE FOR THIS POSITION
"Low man on the scrotum pole."

PSYCHOLOGICAL SIDE EFFECT
Mark claims to have imaginary brother named "Dinky," five minutes younger than him.

DISTURBING REASON TWINS' MOTHER GAVE FOR BELIEVING SECOND-BORN TWIN WAS SPECIAL
As surprise "extra," Mark was God's way of making up for another baby who, years before, had died shortly after birth.

CUTE THROWAWAY CONCERNING AN EYE INFECTION
Mark, historically the less robust and more inclined to childhood ills (standard with second-born twins), is prone to pinkeye at Easter time while Steve is not. Family refers to Mark's affliction as "Easter Bunny Stigmata."

FAVORITE PARTY STUNT AS ADULTS
Half a dozen people, including one twin, go to kitchen and spread mustard on a piece of bread. Anonymous slices presented to other twin, who easily recognizes brothers' spreading style.

REASON TWIN-SPREAD MUSTARD IS EASY TO IDENTIFY
Dense years of proximate art and craft. Side-by-side work in clay, Crayola, and Popsicle sticks. Casual activities of one twin profoundly and involuntarily noted by other. Flourishes in the decoration of ginger-bread men. Relative concavity of foxholes dug in yard for plastic army men. Doodles on fogged-up car windows. Slight angle in hair-brushing style. Distinctive taper at end of straight line drawn with Magic Marker. Inimitable way of denting a pillow or folding a piece of paper in half. The personality in a hung towel. A human universe in an *X* or check mark.

COMPARABLE SIMPATICO RELATIONSHIPS AMONG NON-TWINS
Your spouse, if you've been married thirty years. Maybe.

SOMETHING TWINS HAVE GOING FOR THEM THAT YOU PROBABLY DON'T
Ability to recklessly abuse one's kidneys—knowing an obvious donor is right on hand.

EXASPERATING RESPONSE FROM STRANGERS TO MIDDLE-AGED TWINS
"Ohmigod! You two have *got* to be brothers!"
"Yes. We're twins."
"No. You're not twins."

ROUTINE EXPLANATION FOR WHY ADULT TWINS HAVE GROWN LESS IDENTICAL
"We've been weather-beaten in different ways."

SCARY THING ABOUT HAVING A TWIN AT AGE TEN
Liable to be blamed for twin leaving lids off tempera paints.

SCARY THING ABOUT HAVING A TWIN AT AGE TWENTY
Somebody mad at you for something your twin said to them drunk.

SCARY THING ABOUT HAVING A TWIN AT AGE THIRTY
Sneaking suspicion person on other side of room thinks he or she slept with you.

SCARY THING ABOUT HAVING A TWIN AT AGE FORTY
Seeing age and habit encroach on a three-dimensional, independently mobile likeness of yourself.

WONDERFUL THING ABOUT HAVING A TWIN AT AGE FORTY
Seeing age and habit encroach on a three-dimensional, independently mobile likeness of yourself.

**ASSERTION BY FRIENDS ABOUT O'DONNELL BROTHERS
(RE: FACT THAT THEY NOW LIVE JUST SEVEN BLOCKS APART IN MANHATTAN, AND BOTH WORK AS WRITERS)**
"It's not as creepy as it sounds."

COMPARISON OF GAY AND STRAIGHT TWIN BROTHERS TO SUB-ATOMIC PARTICLES
Exhilarating realization that despite heredity's intractability, environment can interact differently with people just inches away from each other. Every moment, minutely affecting experiences touches us differently, like sub-atomic particles that, completely unpredictably, go one way or another. So for every human, even clones if it comes to that, there is a portion of True Randomness.

**EVERYDAY BENEFIT OF GROWING UP IN HOUSEHOLD OF TEN
BROTHERS AND SISTERS CAPPED BY SET OF TWINS WHO LOVE THE CLEVELAND INDIANS**
Readiness to accept life as a farce.

WHETHER THIS FARCE IS "FUNNY HA-HA" OR "FUNNY STRANGE"
Both, brother. Both.

Front: Stephen and Mark O'Donnell; Back: Mark and Stephen O'Donnell

Photographed by Brian Velenchenko at Dodge Studio in New York City, December 9, 1998.

ukiyo

James Alan McPherson

In early November of 1998, after sustaining a fever for almost two weeks, I developed a case of viral meningitis. This disease attacks the brain by way of the spine and can be fatal, especially to memory. I have been told that Jim Galvin, a friend and a colleague, was sent to my home to see about me when I did not answer my telephone. I am told that he found me unconscious, that he called my physician, Tony Colby, that an ambulance was summoned, and that I was taken to Mercy hospital. There I went into a coma that lasted eleven days. The doctors at Mercy decided that I should be placed in intensive care. But various friends used their influence to have me transferred to the much better-equipped intensive-care unit at University Hospital. When the doctors there determined that I would probably not live, a number of friends called my daughter, at her dorm at Tufts University, and told Rachel that she had better come. Jim Freedman called my sister, Mary, in Stamford, Connecticut, and advised her of my condition. Mary called my brother, Richard, in Atlanta, and advised him to come. Howard, my neighbor across the street, gave my sister a loaf of bread and a quart of fresh milk when she arrived at my home. Howard says that he and Laurel, his wife, watched me carry a suitcase and a video camera to the waiting ambulance.

I do not remember any of it.

When I did regain consciousness, for the very first time in my life I had to rely on *others* to disclose to me my own personal details for nearly two weeks. There was, in my hospital room, a packed suitcase and a video camera that I had borrowed from Rachel earlier in the fall. Jim Galvin told me that when he had found me in my home, I had refused to leave. Perhaps I was so deranged that I could only be convinced to leave if I fantasized that I was going, once again, to see Rachel. Another friend, Fred Woodard, told me that when he visited me in intensive care, I had pleaded with him to help me get out. I had apparently tried to leave so many times that my hands and feet were tied to the bed. Jim Galvin said I called the nurses and doctors "fascist bastards." (a line I remember from Lenny Bruce's routine "White Collar Drunks") when they refused to let me go out for a smoke. Rachel said that I was unconscious most of the time, that I was literally covered with tubes and needles and lights. Rachel said that my eyes were swollen and discolored, and that she recalls my opening them twice. Once was when she and Marian Clark, another friend, were standing outside my room looking at me through a plastic curtain. I opened both my eyes a little and waved both my hands as high as the straps would allow. Rachel said the lights made me look like a Christmas tree. She said I said, "You are so beautiful!" The second time was when Richard was there. Rachel said I opened my swollen eyes as widely as I ever had and stared at Richard. "I guess you opened them so wide because he was standing over you and he is so tall," Rachel told me.

To this day, I have no clear memory of any of it.

Before my illness Richard and I had been estranged for many years. When he called me at my home after my release from University Hospital, he told me, "You have so many friends. I was amazed by all the friends you have out there." And I told Richard, "That's what Daddy always taught us." Our father, James A. McPherson, Sr., had maintained many heartfelt relationships across racial and class lines in tightly segregated Savannah during the forties and fifties. He possessed a generous heart, but liked to drink and gamble, and was always in trouble with the law.

I have two very painful memories of emotional dislocations between Richard and me after our father's death in 1961. The first is from the time of the funeral, a few days after our father died. I was seventeen, Mary was eighteen, Richard was sixteen, and Josephine, our youngest sister, was fourteen. We sat as a family with our mother on a bench in the Sidney A. Jones Funeral Parlor while a minister preached our father's funeral. I can still feel the pain his words inflicted on all of us. He said, "We all knew Mac, and we all know he's better off where he is now." The fact that I walked out of the funeral must have hurt my family, but especially Richard. The second memory derives from a time twenty years later. I had been in his home in Atlanta, and we had had an argument. He had told me, "Remember when I visited you in Berkeley in 1971 and you gave me a reading list? Well, you know what I read? Airplane repair manuals!" And I told him, "Richard, you are an ignorant man."

Richard had ordered me out of his home.

My brother and I grew up together in a segregated Savannah, Georgia. We had enjoyed a thin cushion of middle-class stability early on, when our father worked as an electrical contractor, the only black master electrician, at that time, in the state of Georgia. But he lost his status, as well as control over his life, before Richard and I were adolescents, and the two of us had to go to work to help our mother take care of our two sisters. Richard and I worked very, very hard to get our family off public welfare. In 1961, when I completed high school, I was lucky enough to get a National Defense Student Loan, which enabled me to attend Morris Brown College, a black Methodist College, in Atlanta. In 1962, when he finished high school, Richard joined the Air Force, with ambitions to become a pilot. He visited me once at Morris Brown College before he left for Vietnam. He had been diagnosed as color-blind, so he would not be trained as a pilot. But he later distinguished himself in Vietnam, was promoted in rank, and was able to sit out the last years of the war at an Air Force installation in Athens, Greece.

I have always maintained that there were *two* 1960s, one for black people and another for white people. Simply put, many black people were trying to achieve full citizenship, to get into the mainstream. A lot of young white people, having already experienced the loneliness and the uncertainties of middle-class life, were trying to get out. The black people came from tightly structured communities in which interdependence was essentially a matter of life or death. The white people came out of communities in which the myth of individualism had imposed a norm of habitual suspicion. The white side of this divide was explained to me once, out in Santa Cruz, by a very gentle friend named Don Ferrari, who had been an early inhabitant of the Haight-Ashbury District of San Francisco, before it became a commercial legend. He talked about the spirit of generosity and interdependence that the early residents there tried to achieve. The black side of this spiritual divide, set during this same period and against the very same landscape, was told to me by Anne Thurman, the daughter of Howard Thurman, who was one of Martin Luther King's mentors at Morehouse. Thurman had moved to San Francisco to start his own "universalist" church. His daughter, then a teenager, had found employment in a bank. She had been the only black employee in the bank, and she received what she perceived as brutal treatment. She complained to her father, and the very wise Howard Thurman focused on the inevitable paradox in the quest for greater civil rights. He told her, "Annie, what makes you think that they would treat *you* better than they would treat *each other?*"

Between 1961 and 1971, I had experiences on every level of American society. While in Atlanta, I worked part-time as a waiter at the exclusive Dinkler Plaza Hotel, at the post office, and at the extremely exclusive Piedmont Driving Club (of Tom Wolfe fame) in Buckhead. During the summers I worked as a dining-car waiter on the Great Northern Railroad and was able to explore Chicago, St. Paul and Minneapolis, the Rocky Mountains, and Seattle. I remember watching King's March on Washington, in August of 1963, on a great wall of television sets in a department store in St. Paul. After graduating from Morris Brown, I entered the Harvard Law School. I worked there as a janitor, as a community aide in an Irish-Italian settlement house, and as a research assistant for a professor at the Harvard Business School. I took my law degree and then moved to Iowa City, where I enrolled in the Writers' Workshop. After that I accepted a teaching job at the University of California, moving to Santa Cruz and then later to Berkeley. I published a number of short stories and a book and a series of articles about a Chicago street gang named the Blackstone Rangers, and I'd just completed an essay on Ralph Ellison when my brother and his fiancée visited me, in the fall of 1971, in Berkeley.

Richard and I had experienced very different decades. Returning to Savannah from Athens and Vietnam, he had found employment with Delta Airlines as a mechanic. He moved to Atlanta, where he had met, ten years or so after graduation, a high-school friend named Narvis Freeman who was then working toward her master's degree. He and this hometown girl dated, recognized that they liked each other, and decided to get married.

I know now that, to Richard, I must have seemed a product of the popular images of the 1960s. By this time I *had* inhaled marijuana, but I had not enjoyed it. This was because a gun had been at the back of my head while I inhaled. A Blackstone Ranger was holding the gun while we raced along Lake Shore Drive in Chicago. This had been a test. If I wanted to observe the gang and write about it, the gang had to have something incriminating on me in case I was a narc. The Rangers had their own code. I had also been a draft-dodger. My local board in Savannah had been trying to draft me since my third year in law school. It did not seem to matter to them that Richard was already in Vietnam and that I was enrolled in law school. What seemed, in my own mind, to matter to them was that my name had been listed on the welfare rolls of Chatham County, Georgia, and that I had gotten as far as the Harvard Law School. Given the norms of white supremacy, this must have been considered "wrong." Moreover, on a deeply emotional level, ever since I had walked out on my father's funeral I had kept my vow that no one would ever say over my body that my life had not been worth anything. I had also vowed that I would never allow *any* circumstance to force me into the hands of people who might do me harm, as my father had been done harm. So I remained in school, communicating with my local board from Cambridge, from Iowa City, and from Santa Cruz. Finally, my boss at Santa

Cruz, a writer named James B. Hall, wrote a letter on my behalf to my local board. "You don't want this man," he wrote with his usual irony. "I happen to know that he's crazy." This was sometime in 1970, when the Santa Cruz campus, as well as the campuses of Berkeley, Harvard, Columbia, and Iowa, were exploding with anti-war protests.

But when Richard and Narvis came to visit me in Berkeley in the fall of 1971, I was very much unconscious of my *self*. The only experiences we had in common were our mutual memories of childhood and adolescence in Savannah. We could talk about family matters, about people from back home who were still close to us; but Richard's experience of Southeast Asia and of Athens contained strands of memory so deeply private that they could only be shared, over a great number of years, inside a close relationship like marriage. My own experiences were just as private. But, I still want to believe now, I tried to do the best I could to bridge this gap. I had invited Ishmael Reed to give a talk to my students at Santa Cruz. I invited Richard and Narvis to drive there with us. As I recall, we had a wonderful class. Ishmael was full of gruff humor and street smarts and the students were receptive. When we returned to Berkeley in the evening, the four of us went to a bar and talked some more. Then I invited Richard and his fiancée back to my apartment.

I have now in this house and in my office and in storage close to five thousand books. I left home for college with a single suitcase containing clothes and a National Defense Student Loan. But my love for books had grown the more I read and the more I traveled. When I lived in Cambridge I used to joke that I was amazed to see so many people walking pridefully into bookstores or reading books openly in cafes and restaurants. I noted that, where I came from, such actions constituted an open invitation to be beaten up. As a teacher, books, back then, became my life, an extension of myself. They were a necessity for a very special reason. I had been raised in almost complete segregation, had attended a second- or third-rate college, and had been admitted to the Harvard Law School, where I had been exposed to the legal and intellectual institutions that governed the country. I had left the law school knowing only two levels of the society: the extreme bottom and, much more abstractly, the extreme top. This was still segregation of a kind. Only the experience of reading, I determined, could help me integrate the fuzzy middle area so I could have a complete picture. Paul Freund, who taught me constitutional law at Harvard, used to say that his students knew all the answers without knowing any of the basic questions. I think now that I was trying to learn the basic questions through reading so that, combined with my own experiences, I could develop a national mind—a sense of how the entire culture, regional, ethnic, class, institutional, functioned together, as a *whole*. At the basis of this idea, I concede now, were ideas I had absorbed from conversations with Ralph Ellison and Albert Murray. I know it was this very issue of identity that caused the black 1960s and the white 1960s to come together.

At a time when black nationalist rhetoric had become the new political fashion, I began consciously bonding across racial lines. I thought that the real end of the civil rights movement—beyond economic and political empowerment—needed, if it were to succeed, a moral component that transcended race. It was simply a matter of trying to follow the Golden Rule. This was the open but complex and untested area that lay beyond access to once-closed institutions. It was the human problem raised by Howard Thurman to Annie, his daughter. The search for this moral feeling-tone was what the white 1960s had been all about. It was what Martin King envisioned would happen, would *have* to happen, after the once-closed institutions became open and allowed free-and-easy access to what was unquestionably of transcendent *human* value. These were some of the intellectual abstractions through which I faced my brother in Berkeley that evening in 1971.

I gave him some of my precious books, as I had given books to students and friends for many years before that evening.

Almost ten years later, this time inside Richard's home in Atlanta, the long-delayed confrontation took place. I was then going through a crisis, and it seemed that every place I turned toward those people I had known the longest, there came the same refrain: *remember that time?*, with some inconsequential slight or omission on my part attached to the sound of an old friendship breaking. I managed the crisis as best I could, finally deciding that the only way I could survive, as a whole human being, was to make a break with those people who bore such hidden grudges. This meant, in fact, that I had to make a clear break with an entire region of the country. It meant that I had to turn my back on my entire family. I was willing to pay this price. In about 1992, ten years after I had left the South, two of my Japanese friends were planning to visit Atlanta. I called up Richard, and I asked if he or Narvis, his wife, would greet my two Japanese friends when they arrived at Hartsfield Airport. But Richard told me, "No!" He added, "Remember that ten years ago you drew a line in the sand against the whole South? Well, now I'm drawing a line against *you*! Scratch my name, address, and telephone number out of your address book and never call me here again!"

I know now that Richard had, by this time, good reason for his total dismissal of me. It seems to me now that I had violated the ritual bond that we had shared since childhood. Our mother had been very ill during those ten years, and it had been Richard who had traveled to Savannah each weekend to see about her. It had been Richard who had brought her to Atlanta to see medical specialists. And when she was no longer able to live alone, it had been Richard who had closed down her apartment in Savannah and moved her into his own home in Atlanta. It was Richard who had cooked for her, had given her daily baths and shots of insulin for her diabetes. And it had been Richard who was by her bedside in the hospital when she died.

I recognize, now, that I had dishonored our mother for the sake of a lonely principle, and since those years I have been struggling with what I thought had been vital in that principle. To make this clear, to myself as well as to Richard, and to earn the forgiveness of our mother, I have had to imagine the shadowy dimensions of the William Jefferson Clinton drama that long occupied so much of public discourse. At its basis is the lingering animosity toward those who represented the counter-culture of the 1960s. But there was, and is, something much more subtle at work. King urged us to create a "beloved community," one that intersected, at certain points, with the communal goals of the white counter-culture. Both movements, at their high points, were beginning to formulate an answer to Howard Thurman's question to his daughter, Annie: "What makes you think that they would treat *you* better than they treat *each other*?" Both King and Ghandi, his mentor, would have answered, "Because they have been practicing *swaraj*— self-rule. Because it is only through wishing for the best for others that one can become and remain truly human." Socrates called this special kind of emotional relationship "perfected friendship." The Japanese term relationships that are grounded in such natural feelings *shizen na kamochi*. I believe, in justification of myself, and also of my father, that it is only in locating these emotional resources inside ourselves, as well as inside other people, that one can create meaningful communities, even across racial lines.

The South, as I had experienced it while growing up, and as I had re-experienced it in Charlottesville, Virginia, during the late 1970s and the early 1980s, just did not offer normative opportunities for this kind of human growth. For me, the goal had never been economic success. For me, it had *always* been a matter of personal growth within a communal context unstructured by race. It is a very hard fact of life that there exists no such community in any part of the country. But, at the same time, it *does* exist in every part of the country, among selected individuals from every possible background. But this community is a floating world, the shadowy world that the Japanese name *ukiyo*, sustained, incrementally, by letters, telephone calls, faxes, e-mail, visits from time to time. It is not proximity that keeps it alive, but periodic expenditures of human energy and imagination and grace. This is what I have now, as a substitute for a hometown. I find it more than sufficient.

This is the thing I wanted very badly to explain to Richard, my brother, after I came out of my coma.

After our mother's death Mary, our older sister, began to grow closer to our father's family, the core of which still survives in a little community named Green Pond, South Carolina. Mary began attending reunions there. Then she became active in helping to organize the reunions. Rachel attended one such reunion in Atlanta in the early 1990s, and several years ago I attended another reunion in Detroit. It was a loving affair. Richard was there, and though we were wary of each other, we got along very well. Also attending was my father's half-brother, Thomas McPherson, and his wife, Vanzetta. She is a federal district court judge in Birmingham, Alabama. Thomas's sister, Eva Clayton, was also there. Eva represents a district of North Carolina in the U.S. Congress. There was no sense of rank or of status among us. We were simply family, simply community. When I began telling jokes, Eva told me that I should never call her up in Washington, as I had habitually called up Mary in Stamford, to recite my latest one-liners. She said that they might, if overheard, get her in trouble.

We took a group trip deep into Windsor, Canada, across the river from Detroit, in order to visit a station on the old Underground Railroad. The tour guide detailed the complex history of this station, one grounded in a communal effort that had transcended race. He noted that a great number of wooden carts, piled high with manure used for fertilizer, would stop periodically at the station. And hidden in the false bottom of those carts, beneath the great piles of manure, would be fugitive slaves. We were all in good spirits, so I decided to try a one-liner on Richard. I said, "Richard, those carts are the ritual basis of our old Negro expression, 'Nigger you ain't shit!' Only we have forgotten the celebratory tone that used to go with it. Our fugitive slave ancestors really said when they opened those false bottoms, 'Nigger, you *ain't* shit. *You're a free man!*'"

Richard laughed then, and the years of ice began to melt.

Last year Mary attended another reunion, again with members of our father's family, in Patterson, New Jersey. She sent me a news article about one of the young men descended from this line, who, Mary says, is our third cousin. His name is Leonard Brisbon. He is a major in the Air Force and is the co-pilot of Air Force One. He is an honors graduate of the Air Force Academy and has won many awards. In the article he talked about his parents and their values, and about his family roots in Green Pond, South Carolina. His lifelong ambition, he said, was to go to Mars. I plan to travel to the next reunion of this branch of my family, no matter where it takes place, in order to meet this cousin. I hope that Richard will also be there. I know he would be very proud of how high this cousin in our family had risen in the Air Force. In the meantime, I am practicing a new one-liner, one that I plan to try on Leonard Brisbon. I plan to say to him, "You crazy Negro. There ain't no collard greens on Mars!" I am hoping that Leonard Brisbon will laugh, along with Richard. I hope both of them will be able to accept me as I am.

I also hope to have a much better funeral than my father had.

Portfolio II

Dan Patrick, 42, sportscaster; Mike Pugh, 46, advertising executive; Dave Pugh, 38, radio station general manager; Bill Pugh, 44, sports radio operations director

"Our relationship is as good as it gets. As we've moved on in our lives and careers, it gets tougher to find the time to just hang out and be ourselves. But when we do get together, all the urgency and the stress is gone, and the pace just slows down, we get very relaxed, just shoot the shit. We enjoy giving each other shit—giving it and taking it."
—Bill Pugh

Photographed by Edward Gajdel in Mason, Ohio, November 27, 1998.

Marty Zeiger, 61, attorney, pharmaceutical executive; Larry King, 65, talk show host

"For a long time now we've been very close. We're friends as much as brothers. But when we were kids we didn't spend much time together—he didn't want me tagging along when he was with his friends. Once when he was about 14 and I was 10, my mother insisted he take me along to a ball game at Ebbets Field. At one point in the game, I was looking around for him in the stadium, and then I spotted him in the front row of the bleachers, his score card rolled up into a cone. He was speaking into it, announcing the game. He emulated Red Barber while the rest of us emulated Duke Snider." —**Marty Zeiger**

Photographed by Harry Benson in McLean, Virginia, November 21, 1998.

Nick Fish, 40, attorney; Hamilton Fish, 47, political consultant; Peter Fish, 39, Americorps project director

For four successive generations, Hamilton Fishes served in Congress as Republicans representing New York's Hudson Valley. The first Hamilton Fish was also a Senator and Governor from New York and served President Grant as his Secretary of State. His grandson was a conservative lion and a constant thorn in the side of Franklin Roosevelt. Elected to Congress in 1922, he was an early anti-Communist, a vigorous opponent of the New Deal, and a leading isolationist until the day following the Japanese attack on Pearl Harbor. The patrician cadences of FDR's popular refrain, "Martin, Barton, and Fish," helped define the pre-war era. His son, the fourth Hamilton Fish to serve in Congress, retired in 1994 after twenty-six years in office. A moderate and the ranking member of the House Judiciary Committee, he was revered by colleagues on both sides for his bipartisan stewardship of civil rights, voting rights, and the needs of the disabled.

The present generation of Fishes has contributed a dramatic twist to the family tradition of public service. Whether it was the legacy of Watergate (in which their father played a pivotal role), or the influence of Communists at Harvard College (as suggested by their grandfather), each of the new generation of Fishes departed from established family tradition and became a Democrat.

Nick worked on Barney Frank's first Congressional campaign. Peter is an expert on volunteerism and is establishing an Albany office of the AmeriCorps program. Ham, who has made two unsuccessful bids for Congress, is the former publisher of *The Nation* and a producer of documentary films, including the Academy Award-winning *Hotel Terminus*.

Photographed by Brad Wilson at Fraunces Tavern in New York City, January 30, 1999.

Eric Tilford, 30, designer; Todd Tilford, 35, writer and designer; Keith Tilford, 33 design marketing director
"Talking to one of us is like talking to two of us is like talking to three of us. I can't remember a time when we really disagreed about anything. It's actually kind of terrifying." —Eric Tilford

Photographed by John Huet outside Phoenix, Arizona, February 27, 1999.

Terrance Morgan, 49; Lewis Morgan, 55; and Ronald Morgan, 47; furniture caners

They were teenagers when a doctor told their father that new eyeglasses wouldn't help, that his three sons would go blind, completely and quickly. Lewis and Ronald soon dropped out of school. Terrance learned how to cane chairs from a blind woman, and he taught his brothers how to mount the frames and string the rattan strips—cross-weave, snowflake, seven-step—guiding the patterns by feel. They live in the house where they grew up and fix chairs for their younger brother Gregory, who has normal vision and owns a woodworking shop next door. Lewis and Ronald share a bed. After dinner, they crowd into Terrance's room, turn on the radio, and listen to the Red Sox game. "If we argue, it's mostly about sports," Terrance says. "But we do whatever we can for each other, and it's been that way from the start."

Photographed by John Huet in Gregory Morgan's shop, outside Providence, Rhode Island, April 2, 1998.

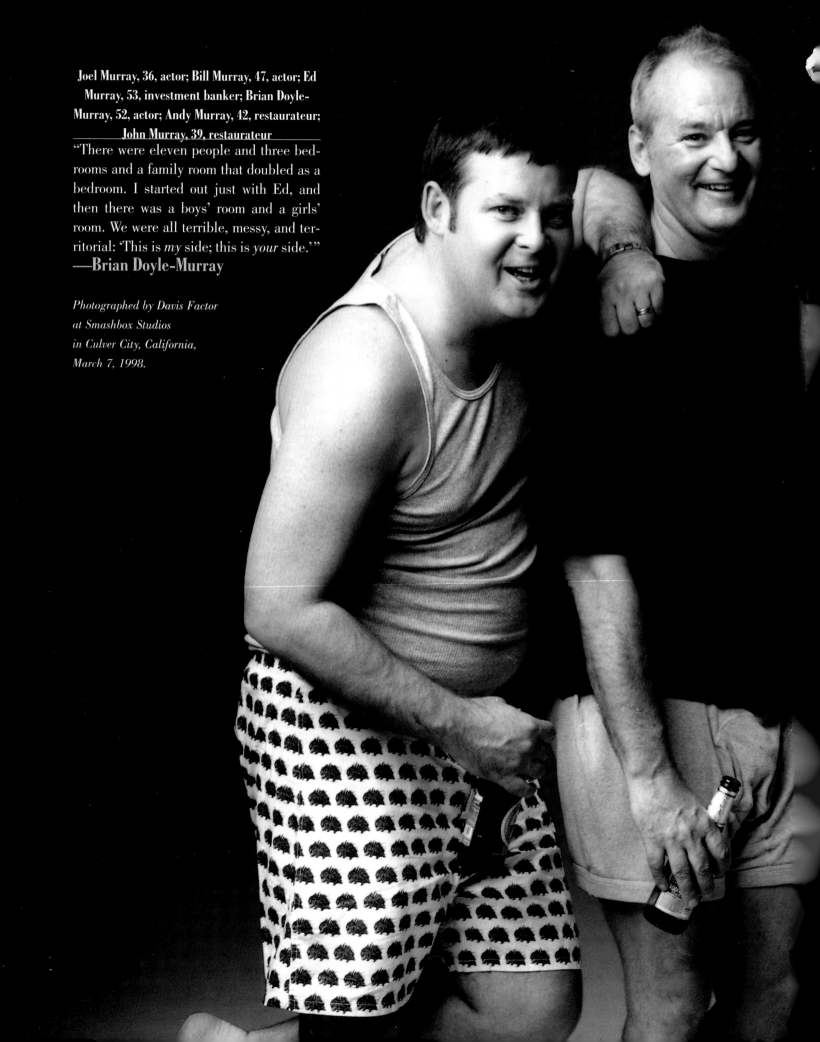

Joel Murray, 36, actor; Bill Murray, 47, actor; Ed Murray, 53, investment banker; Brian Doyle-Murray, 52, actor; Andy Murray, 42, restaurateur; John Murray, 39, restaurateur

"There were eleven people and three bedrooms and a family room that doubled as a bedroom. I started out just with Ed, and then there was a boys' room and a girls' room. We were all terrible, messy, and territorial: 'This is *my* side; this is *your* side.'"
——**Brian Doyle-Murray**

Photographed by Davis Factor
at Smashbox Studios
in Culver City, California,
March 7, 1998.

<u>Dexter Scott King, 37; Martin Luther King III, 40</u>
"No matter what [Martin] does, where he goes, people are going to rally around the name,"
Dexter King said recently. "He has had a very challenging road to travel because he does carry the name.
He has a much greater burden than I do."

Photographed by Andrew French at the King Center in Atlanta, April 9, 1998.

Leslie and Leigh Keno, 41, antiques experts

The Keno brothers are best known for their regular appearances on PBS's *Antiques Roadshow*. Raised in upstate New York, they developed their interest in antiques at an early age, following their parents to antique shows and flea markets in the region. By the time they were twelve, the two had started their own business, collecting late-eighteenth- and nineteenth-century ceramic jugs and pots. Selling off the collection was difficult but necessary when they got older—it helped pay for college—but they have recently tried to buy back some of the old pieces. The pot they hold in the photograph is one of those venerable pieces—crafted by John Remmey, a late-eighteenth-century potter from Manhattan. "Leslie and I are probably as close as two brothers can be," says Leigh Keno. "We're best friends as much as brothers."

Photographed by Karen Kuehn at Leigh Keno American Antiques in New York City, December 10, 1998.

**Bob Weinstein, 43, and Harvey Weinstein, 46,
co-chairmen of Miramax Films**

"When was the last time we fought? Every day. We
always did, and we thought that everybody else did.
We're only just really learning to keep it down. Not
between us, but with everybody else. Because our dad
taught us fight and forget, fight and forgive. Fight for
what you believe in—then two seconds later, it's your
brother. But I see that's not the philosophy everybody
else grew up with." —**Harvey Weinstein**

*Photographed by Danny Clinch at the Tribeca Film Center in
New York City, March 10, 1998.*

wandering home

Scott Anderson

At first glance, it might seem odd that my brother and I were looking for the missing bodies of different dead men at the same time. Actually, I think there was a certain inevitability to it. I believe I can even pinpoint the conversation that set our parallel quests in motion. It had come some thirteen years beforehand, on a hot afternoon in mid-August 1982, while we lolled in the shallow end of an apartment complex swimming pool in Washington, D.C., surrounded by plastic replicas of Greek statuary and extraordinarily old people. I was twenty-three, a frustrated novelist turned bartender, and my brother, Jon Lee, was twenty-five, a fledgling reporter. He had recently moved to Washington after several years in South America, and I attributed his choice of living quarters—an apartment high-rise in the far reaches of northwest Washington with a median resident age of about eighty-seven—to his being completely out of touch with American culture.

Over the course of an hour or so of wallowing in the pool, Jon Lee mapped out a golden future for the two of us. We would escape from our current mundane circumstances by teaming up and roaming the globe in search of adventure and publishable stories. We would journey to the world's best and worst places—its uncharted jungles and deserts, its battlefields and lost civilizations—write about them, then move on to the next frontier. We would stay in near constant motion, only returning to the States when absolutely necessary, to schmooze with editors, cash our checks.

Jon Lee was always more of a dreamer than I, but on that day I got caught up in his vision. It was only after some time that I detected an overlooked detail in the grand scheme.

"Sounds great," I said, "but what do we do about them?"

I cocked my head toward the only two other under-eighties at poolside, my live-in girlfriend, and my brother's wife of one year, chatting and tanning on nearby chaise lounges. Jon Lee turned and stared at them with a perplexed frown.

"What," he finally asked, "you think they'd mind?"

"I don't know," I said, "women are funny."

We had had exciting, exotic childhoods—maybe a little too exciting. The sons of an agricultural adviser for the American government, we had grown up in east Asia, our exposure to the United States largely limited to brief "home leave" visits until our teen years. "Home leave" was a kind of government-imposed vacation in which the families of American officials abroad had to return to the United States for two months every two years to re-acquaint themselves with their native country, but in our case, there had been nothing to re-acquaint with, no ancestral home to return to, and the States had always felt as alien a place as any other. When we did finally move to the United States for good in the mid-1970s, it was too late for assimilation. I managed to stick it out through high school before embarking on a nomadic existence, but my brother didn't even manage that; by seventeen, he was off—to Europe, to Africa, finally to South America.

Somehow our three sisters, raised the same rootless way, escaped all this. They seemed to possess a resourcefulness, a homing instinct, that had passed us by. Our sisters were able to settle down, become members of communities, and for both Jon Lee and myself their skill at doing so was both a source of amazement and quiet envy. By contrast, we seemed joined together in the most quixotic of missions: to constantly search for that place we might call home, while remaining profoundly reluctant to ever find it. By that August afternoon in the Washington, D.C., geriatric pool, my brother and I had both carved out patinas of domesticity for ourselves—apartments, jobs, de facto or real spouses—but I'm quite sure that if either of us had had enough money for plane tickets, we would have been gone by nightfall. Shortly after, however, the pendulum abruptly swung back the other way.

On a cold, gray day that autumn, Jon Lee enthusiastically bushwhacked through the tangled underbrush and dead leaves of West Virginia hillside. Several weeks before, in a sudden homesteading fever, he had bought ten acres of mountain scrubland outside the town of Romney for $5,000, and had spent much of the intervening time relating in excruciating detail his plans for the place. On this day, the two of us had finally made the drive out from Washington to look the property over.

Reaching the top of the hill, the land opened out into a small plateau, rocky and studded with bare wintered trees.

"This is where the house will go," Jon Lee said, sweeping a hand over the expanse. "Two stories, a big porch coming out this way so you get the southern exposure." He led the way farther along the hilltop, to where the land dropped down onto a smaller plateau. "And this is where we'll build the office—two big rooms, one for each of us, a common den in between with a huge fireplace."

For perhaps twenty minutes, Jon Lee described precisely how our home in the West Virginia woods would look; in his mind it was already built. When he was done, he gazed happily over the cascading slopes of trees, then turned to me.

"So, what do you think?" he asked. "It'll be a kind of home base for us. We can go hunting, fishing. It'll be great."

I was tempted to point out that both of us were broke, that neither of us were hunters, that we both loathed fishing, that the nearest outpost of civilization was a pizzeria in Romney with a disquieting sign in the window that read "our pizzas are made with real cheese." But one of the unspoken arrangements between us was to never disparage the other's plans or hopes for settling down; for both of us, it was important to maintain the idea that we might change. Instead, I nodded and mimicked his appreciative gaze over the surrounding mountains.

"Very cool," I said. "Very, very cool."

The house in West Virginia was never built. In fact, neither Jon Lee or I ever visited the land again.

If not to our ambitious timetable or precise specifications, both Jon Lee and I steadily fell sway to the plan concocted in the swimming pool that day. By the summer of 1983, he had signed on with *Time* magazine and left for the battlefields of Central America. After a five-month ramble through Europe, I went to war-torn Beirut in a futile effort to find a job that would keep me there. We wrote one book together and, in the summer of 1986, set out to do another: an oral history of modern war. For nearly a year we came close to living the lives we had imagined in the swimming pool, except we weren't going to the world's best places, only the worst, roaming over five continents, dropping into one war zone for a month or so before moving onto the next. Constant companions, we became like an old married couple, able to read each other's moods probably better than our own. There were times when we annoyed each other, of course, but there were also times when we had close calls, and these times deepened our inseparability, the sense that we only had each other to rely on.

At the end of that year, we found ourselves in a small town in southern Spain, contemplating what came next. Nothing leapt immediately to mind, for now we didn't even have ersatz homes to return to; in recent weeks, both Jon Lee's wife and my girlfriend had decided they'd had enough of our ceaseless wanderings and long absences, and simultaneously given us the boot.

"I don't know what the problem was," Jon Lee said, genuinely puzzled. "I mean, it's not like we were gone *that* long."

"I told you women are funny," I replied.

It was our last night together—Jon Lee was flying out to Central America in the morning, I was staying in Spain for a while—and we were sitting in a cafe-bar.

"So, where do you think you'll go to live?" he finally asked.

I thought about it for a long time, couldn't come up with an answer.

"Whole lot of options; what about you?"

Jon Lee shrugged.

As soon as he walked through the door of my apartment, I could tell that Jon Lee was appalled. There was a lot to be appalled by.

After our parting in Spain, I'd returned to the States and, in that tricky confluence where whimsy meets despair, had decided to forge a new home for myself in Baltimore, a place where I knew no one and that I had only previously glimpsed from the Interstate. When I'd first moved into the three-bedroom apartment in the Fells Point neighborhood, I'd been flush with plans; I was going to repaint the place, buy furniture, make new friends. That enthusiasm had lasted a good three days. In the intervening six months, I had only managed to amass a futon bed, a small table, one chair, and an eight-foot plastic marlin that I had found in the trash, and all of this was crowded into the front bedroom; the other two bedrooms I used as my dirty-clothes piles, one room for whites, the other for colors. I had met no one in Baltimore, had made no effort to, and was desperate to escape.

But this was something I couldn't admit to Jon Lee and, as obvious as it must have been, not something he would comment on. Instead, he wandered appraisingly through the cavernous place, gazed out the dirty front windows to the grim street.

"Very nice, man." He nodded approvingly. "I've always heard great things about Baltimore."

Despite our joint quest, there had always been at least one key difference between Jon Lee and myself; he was a collector of things, I had an almost phobic reaction to possessions. By the late 1980s, he had completely filled an eight-by-twelve storage shed in Washington with artifacts he had gathered in his travels; the spillover was filling up the closets of a half-dozen friends across the United States and Europe. He talked of gathering all these things in one place, of one day going through the contents of the storage shed, with the same wistful, hopeful tone that accompanied our frequent home-hunting conversations.

By then, I could still comfortably fit all my worldly belongings into the trunk and back seat of a very small car. Whatever rudimentary furniture I needed I picked up at garage sales or off the street, and it all went back on the street when I decided it was time to move on. My asceticism had been periodically assisted by high-tempered girlfriends and house fires. Twice, domestic misunderstandings had resulted in most of my possessions being tossed onto city sidewalks, the excess further reduced in the mid 1980s when the restaurant I lived above in Charlottesville, Virginia, caught fire.

"Why would you ever live above a restaurant?" my brother asked me at the time. "They burn down all the time."

By 1990, after my homesteading fiasco in Baltimore and a couple of years in Boston, I found myself in Iowa. No conflagration had come my way for some time, my current girlfriend was unusually placid, and my belongings had expanded to an alarming degree; recalling my brother's old observation, it seemed a good time to move above another restaurant. It took nearly a year for that restaurant to catch fire. When it did, I sat on the opposite curb, watched the smoke billowing from my apartment windows, and thought, "now that's spring cleaning."

At least on the surface, Jon Lee was making a much better go of things. By then, he had remarried, begun having children, was residing in a thatched cottage in the English countryside outside Oxford. Of course, *residing* was a relative term; he was now writing a book about guerrilla groups around the world, spending eight or nine months a year on the road. When I flew over to England to visit him, he had only been back from one war zone or another for a few days. We took a long walk through the bucolic village, he pointed out the local landmarks—churches, manor houses—and there seemed about him such a sense of contentment that I was moved to ask if this was the place, if it was here in the pastoral England that he would finally put down stakes.

"Are you kidding?" he said. "I'm going crazy here."

Shortly after, Jon Lee set to work on a biography of the Marxist revolutionary Che Guevara. Che had been executed by Bolivian soldiers in 1967 and his body disappeared along with those of a dozen companions, but by the spring of 1995, my brother had cajoled a retired Bolivian general into revealing the location of the secret graves, sparking a massive exhumation project at a remote airstrip in the Andes. At the same time, I was in Chechnya searching for an American disaster relief expert named Fred Cuny who had vanished with three companions. I'm not sure that either Jon Lee or I consciously set out with the idea that we might actually find these missing men, but for both of us that became the goal.

Che Guevara had left his native Argentina when he was seventeen and had wandered aimlessly throughout Latin America before finding his place alongside Fidel Castro in the Cuban revolution. Fred Cuny was from Texas, but he had spent twenty-five years roaming the globe in endless search of the next disaster zone. Che had only returned to his homeland once as a grown man; Cuny returned to his Dallas home a few weeks each year, but invariably became restless and set off again. I think both Jon Lee and I caught glimpses of ourselves in these rootless, stateless men. Even if we seemed incapable of finding a place to call home, it would feel good to return these lost men to theirs.

I was unable to recover Cuny's body—it remains somewhere on the battlefield of Chechnya—but Jon Lee's quest was more successful; after months of digging on the Bolivian airstrip, Che's skeleton was finally found.

This most famous prodigal son of Argentina was not returned to his homeland, however. Instead, he was carried off to Cuba, his tiny boxed coffin wrapped in a Cuban flag, his remains carried through the streets of Havana in a solemn Cuban state funeral. When I commented on the irony of this, Jon Lee shrugged, "Well, he had to end up somewhere."

Jon Lee's call from Missoula came late one night in the spring of 1998. He sounded dispirited. For at least the past five years, Jon had talked of moving to Montana with his second wife and their three children. It was there, in the great expanse of the American West, that he would finally put down roots, where his children would grow up with a sense of belonging and home that neither he nor I had ever known. And, of course, it wasn't just for his children; Jon Lee wanted to be a part of a landscape, as well.

The one potential snag in this plan, as I had gently pointed out on several occasions, was that he had never actually been to Montana. Now, in 1998, he had carved out a week from his schedule and finally flown out to see his Shangri-La.

"So, how is it?" I asked.

"It sucks." For the next twenty minutes, Jon Lee railed on about how Montana had been destroyed, covered with trailer parks and forty-acre ranchettes, how there were people and strip-malls everywhere, how he could never imagine living there.

I listened to him in silence, sitting in my apartment in Brooklyn. I had lived there for four years, the longest I'd ever lived anywhere, but I'd yet to put anything on the walls, there was one chair in the whole place, and I kept my passport in plain view on the bookcase.

After Jon Lee had talked himself out, I wanted to say, "well, what did you expect?" But I didn't. The old unspoken arrangement between us still existed, we had to maintain the idea that this home thing might yet work out. Instead, I shifted the conversation, started talking up the latest place I was considering: upstate New York.

"Just two or three hours from the city and you can be in total wilderness," I said. "There's great cross-country skiing, snowmobiling, ice-fishing." I listed two or three other activities that neither of us had ever done, that we'd never shown the slightest interest in doing.

By the end of my pitch, Jon Lee's mood had brightened dramatically. "It sounds perfect," he said. "Let me know what you find up there."

brotherless

Charles P. Pierce

I am the son of a brother and of someone who had brothers. I am the father of brothers and of people who have brothers. They are what I am not. I am not a brother and I have no brothers. I am an only child. I did not have brothers, so I went out and made friends. Most of them were brothers to someone, and I met the brothers, too. They mystified me, communicating at times in a strange, elliptical way, words unspoken, but understood. I could not communicate in this way—code-talking, blood-speech, words dropping out but thoughts still passing, one to the other. I kept up as best I could.

I know what I am supposed to be—self-centered, ego-driven, unable to work and play well with others. I am supposed to be like this because I was deprived of so many of childhood's formative arguments. I grew up in a world without comparison. I had no immediate examples against which to measure myself—the way my father had, the way all my children do. I learned that the world was wider through my own experience, and not from the living, breathing, snoring evidence across the room —which also was the living, breathing, snoring evidence that, yes, my parents . . . had sex! Which was something I had to surmise from my own existence. I walked through a mysterious world of unspoken bonds and quick passions, learning on my own what brothers seem to know from birth and in the blood. Luckily, as it turns out, I am not entirely self-centered, far from the most ego-driven person I know, and much better able now to work and play well with others.

Things are looking up.

There was something I learned very recently about being an only child. Not long ago, two of my friends lost their brothers. One of them died in a highway accident. The other was taken by a swift cancer. Sudden, blind deaths, the two of them. Through these deaths, I learned that not all only children are born only children, like me. Some only children are made.

I did not know the first one, except through a picture that hangs in a saloon not far from the backside of the famous left field wall at Fenway Park. My friend pointed his brother out to me. There he was, captured forever right in the heart of a joyous mob come out of the stands to celebrate the Red Sox's improbable 1967 American League pennant. He is not far from the mound, rushing toward an old Boston pitcher named Jim Lonborg. I remember that day, more than thirty years ago, when the Sox clinched the pennant. My best friend (a brother to two sisters) had come running over to my house from next door. Now, however, that day is different in my memory because of that picture on the wall of a Boston saloon; because of the man in it, whom I met only through his brother's memory of the joy of that sharp-shadowed autumn afternoon.

The other brother who died, that one I knew, and he was one of the finest men I ever met. He was a combat aviator in Vietnam, where he had the charming job of refueling bombers over enemy airspace. He came home, married, and he had two daughters. He was cheery and he was wise, and we talked about running him for Congress one day. One evening, my friend told me that his brother had cancer. Later, but not much later, my friend told me that his brother had died. I went to the wake and to the funeral, and I watched my friend working the room in his grief, the way that the Irish have done for longer than the collective memory holds. I realized at that moment that my friend now had to learn to be what I was, and what he never had been. He had to learn how to be an only child.

It was too late for him to learn to be self-centered, ego-driven, and unable to work and play well with others. He had been a brother too long for that. He had been shaped already by so many of childhood's formative arguments ("You got more presents at Christmas than I did." "How come I have to pick up your socks?" "You going out with her again?"), arguments that I had missed because I had no one to have them with, except my parents, which hardly counts.

But, if I had missed all of them, my friend had missed the lessons of being an only child, and now he had to learn them on the fly. He had to learn how to be the focus of his family's future. He had to learn how to react when his mother became curious about his work and his life, and now there was nobody else talking when he was finished. He had known from the start, in his blood, what I had come to learn for myself—that he was part of something larger. He had lived a history that ran on dual tracks, twining together as they moved forward, and now one of those tracks had stopped, and only his was moving forward through the rest of his life, alone.

Are you still a brother to someone if that person dies? Does the history move forward with the surviving brother, the two tracks now twisted together by cruel circumstance until the history of the brother now gone disperses completely in the life of the brother who remains, like a stormfront thinned by the altitude winds? How do Edward Kennedy and young Joseph Kennedy—both brothers to two brothers who died young—define themselves without the people who helped define them? How do they get out of bed in the morning? These are not my questions, and I do not know the beginnings of the answers to them.

I am brother to nobody and nobody's brother. Except metaphorically, of course. We are all brothers, according to Jesus of Nazareth. Of course, if you believe some of the early Gospels, He had some brothers Himself; a fellow named James the Just was said to have been one of them. However, through centuries of tricky translation, the brothers of Jesus have been disappeared, perhaps to surpress the walking evidence that Joseph and Mary did the wild thing for reasons other than the redemption of sinful man. But imagine the arguments around a certain Nazarene family carpentry firm, as some of the sons sweat over tables and chairs while their brother walks the God-thick hills, each of them plagued with the question that has plagued generations of brothers, another of the questions never asked of me, an only child:

"Why can't you be more like your brother?"

Just to keep the record straight, my mother was an only child, and so was her mother, and I do in many ways tend toward that side of the family. (There exists an old studio portrait taken of my maternal grandmother that my wife insists looks exactly like me in Hibernian debutante drag, but that is only because it does.) I watched the brothers I knew growing up, and I parceled them out between their parents, always assuming (as an only child will) that I'd gotten all the best and worst of both of mine. I wondered about primal jealousies, if the brothers argued at some fathomless level over who got the best parts of their parents, the way they would argue about who got the best presents at Christmastime. They were not my arguments, but I wondered just the same.

I have watched brothers all my life. I watched them in my family growing up, and I watch my children today, the blood-speech of the code-talkers in the other bedrooms, the swift bursts of anger and the reconciliations, all operating on rules as foreign and distant to me as Hammurabi's Code. It is a world of brothers in which I live, an only child. They are what I am not.

Often I am asked by people who are not only children if I feel as though I've been cheated. My answer is always twofold: (1) that I really didn't have much choice in the matter, and (2) that I defined myself alone as easily as my friends who were brothers defined themselves as such. I didn't miss anything because, as Muddy Waters so elegantly put it, you can't spend what you ain't got, and you can't lose what you never had. Fairness doesn't enter into it. I think back, then, to my friend, working the room at his brother's wake, and I think that he was the one who was cheated, that no brother should ever have to learn how to be an only child, and that, in a just world, only children would only be born, never made.

we happy few

Joseph P. Kennedy II

It usually happens at a party or some event—I know very well I should be out shaking hands, meeting people. But inevitably I find myself surrounded by my brothers. I am drawn to them. It is where there is life. It is where I feel most alive.

And so there we stand in a group of two or three or four or more. The conversation is fast and fun. One of us is telling a story, possibly an adventure—how my brother Max recently engineered a diving expedition off the coast of Venezuela in search of a three-hundred-year-old shipwreck; how he was dragged a mile over a dangerous reef by a strong current; how the rest of us saw a picture of him in the newspaper and thought he looked as though he could have been a crew member of the original sunken boat. Or the talk is self-deprecating—how for the first twenty-five years of my life I thought I was the best athlete in the family, but now we all agree that for the last twenty I've been steadily declining to the worst. Everyone laughs, Douglas claps his hands. Bobby drives the point home.

One of us has his arm resting on another's shoulder. He pushes off when a punch line is reached. All of us are grinning, clapping in appreciation, waiting in anticipation for what will be said next. I can sense other people's amusement, enjoying our camaraderie. At moments like these, I realize how much I love my brothers.

I remember when Michael died. It wasn't until the next day, when I found myself in an upstairs bedroom in Hyannis Port with my brothers Max, Douglas, Chris, and Bobby and our sister Rory, that I realized he was truly gone.

On the hour-and-a-half drive carrying Michael's body from the funeral home in Hyannis Port to the cemetery in Brookline, we were told there was room for only one of us in the hearse. But all of us ended up going. Bobby and I squeezed into the front seat with the driver; in the back, Max, Douglas, and Chris scrunched in next to Michael's coffin. The mass had been tearful. Bobby and I had both eulogized Michael. But now, in the car, the conversation was full of the great fun Michael was to us. We all laughed heartily, unfettered. A windowed partition between the front and the back muffled some of the conversation, and each of us kept pushing it back and forth in order to hear the stories better.

It is not simply that I feel close to my brothers and my sisters (in our family, they're honorary brothers, or maybe we're honorary sisters); it's that I feel most truly myself when I'm around them.

When I think of David, Michael, Max, Bobby, Douglas, and Christopher, or when I think of my father and his brothers, Teddy, Jack, and Joe, I'm reminded of that line from Shakespeare: "We few, we happy few, we band of brothers."

The sons of Robert F. Kennedy,
(clockwise from top)
Douglas Kennedy, 31,
TV news correspondent;
Christopher Kennedy, 34,
corporate executive;
Joseph P. Kennedy II, 45, politician;
Max Kennedy, 33, teacher;
Robert F. Kennedy Jr., 44, attorney

*Photographed by Max Vadukul at Chelsea
Piers in New York City, March 24, 1998.*

there will be talk

Frank McCourt

There are pictures to prove that the four McCourt brothers assembled on the 5th of September, 1996, at Ireland House, Fifth Avenue, for the launch of *Angela's Ashes*, a memoir of our collective miserable childhood in Ireland. There we are, gray and/or white, sliding into the high-maintenance stage of life. There we are, Frank, Malachy, Mike, Alphie in descending order of age and ascending order of common sense. We're with our nearest and dearest, we're in suits and ties, we radiate the well-scrubbed look butter wouldn't melt. After I read an excerpt from the book each of the brothers says something and we sing "Barefoot Days," a kind of family anthem.

You'd never guess from these pictures that we hadn't all been together at once in the same room since Christmas, 1966. You'd never guess how careful we were to avoid a repeat of that night of hard words that hurt and flying fists that never found their target. A student of racial stereotypes might have said, "Ah, the Irish. They're at it again with the drinking and brawling. Excuse me, is this a private fight or can anyone get into it?"

Only Malachy escaped that fateful evening. He had dropped in earlier with his wife, Diane, and her parents, John and Berenice. They said how nice everything was: the tree topped with a sweet little white angel; the cat wandering around with his little red Christmas bow on his neck; the aroma of a standing three-rib roast beef wafting from the kitchen; my wife, Alberta, dispensing drinks and appetizers; my mother arriving with her Swiss friend, Violet. "Very nice," said John and Berenice to Malachy. "Such a pleasure to see people enjoying Christmas and each other." They were sorry they had to go to another Christmas dinner. Wished they could have stayed with us, so comfortable, warm, relaxed. Maybe next year.

They left as the Clancy brothers were arriving, the brothers at the height of their fame—Paddy, Tom, Liam. My brother, Mike, came in with his wife, Donna, and Alphie trailed behind them, alone. It was, Hi, lovely tree, brought you something, have a drink. It was, Hi, God that smells good, I'm starved, yeah, I'd sure love a drink.

I look back on that night and realize that most of our guests had already imbibed on empty stomachs and that might explain the little brotherly brush fires. Certain guests were already snapping at each other (hunger? thirst? Christmas?) and my brothers and I began taking sides. Alphie erupted, "I hate all this family fighting, the four of us always fighting. There's always one fighting the other three or two fighting the other two and I'm sick of it, sick of it." It was admirable the way he sorted out the mathematics of the thing and to prove it he brought his fist down on a shelf of precious cargo—scotch, Irish, vodka, gin—which went crashing to the floor and when I said, "For Christ's sake, Alphie," brother Mike sprang to his defense, told me to get off Alphie's back. I invited him outside, where we were about to go at it when a car filled with jeering Christmas revelers so enraged us we chased it down the street till it went through a red light and we lost it and forgot what we were fighting about and returned to the apartment singing "Silent Night."

My wife, Alberta, barked at me that I had no business leaving the party like that when she was having so much trouble with one of the guests rolling around the floor there in some kind of fit. Brother Mike joked that the guest was probably hungry and I took him seriously and knelt on the floor offering her a roast beef sandwich. Tom Clancy said, "What the hell are you doing giving a roast beef sandwich to someone in the throes of an epileptic fit?" and his brother, Paddy, said, "When did you become an expert on epileptic fits?" and that led to another sibling battle, Clancy style, with Liam strumming away on his guitar and singing "The Leaving of Liverpool."

There was a yelp from the living room and Mike said, "You gotta see this." What I had to see was my mother's friend, Violet, on her back under a fallen Christmas tree, cursing the cat who was in a corner pawing and chewing on the little white angel, which he had captured by somehow knocking over the tree. Mike lifted the tree and I helped Violet back to the couch beside my mother, where Violet said, "Ve don't do this kind of thing in Switzerland. Ve sit under the tree and sing Christmas carols," and my mother said, "We sing Christmas carols, too, and then beat the shit out of each other."

People were already leaving the party, expressing their dismay over our uncouth behavior, all of us, the whole McCourt family, and that other gang, the Clancys. People were saying, Well, I never, and promising never to return and that was okay with me because the apartment looked like a war zone. How was I to know that when Michael left, shaking his head, we four brothers would drift so far apart geographically and every other way that we wouldn't be in the same room again for another thirty years?

Writing about my brothers is a dangerous occupation, dancing through a minefield. They talk about me: I know they do. Alphie was right. Two of us will talk about the other two and three will talk about one. When we learn that Mike drove his car into a wall in San Francisco we say, "What the hell is he thinking of, driving his car into a wall?" Or if we hear Alphie didn't drive his car into a wall anywhere we might say, "What the hell is he thinking of, not driving his car into a wall?"

It doesn't matter what you do or don't do: there will be talk.

In the matter of drink I have to be careful. I could avoid the topic altogether but it's there, like Catholicism and dandruff, and all I want to do is rise up and tell the world I have three brothers who don't touch a drop. I'm saying this and living dangerously, because one or more of said brothers will bark in high dudgeon, "What the hell. We've done other things in life besides not drink," and I whimper because when they don the mantle of dudgeon they can be fearsome.

I touch a drop myself, a little wine with dinner, as they say, not because I love the stuff but because it gives work, keeps people employed, enables decent men and women to buy shoes and birthday gifts for their loved ones. My brothers take a dim view of my philanthropic nature, of course, and ask why I can't bestow money directly, and I can only reply that their sobriety has rendered them clear-headed beyond my understanding.

Malachy and Alphie have lived for decades on the Upper West Side of Manhattan, Mensa plateau, and the neighborhood does things to you. (Disclaimer: I've moved to the Upper West Side myself and await the moment of enlightenment.) My brothers Malachy and Alphie might have a greater appetite for tofu than Mike and I. They've been advocating and practicing yoga for years and are drawn spiritually more to the foot of the Himalayas than to the altars of Rome. I'm more of a Rome man myself. I don't know where Mike stands, though I have a feeling he doesn't give a fiddler's fart.

My brother Alphie may be the only Irishman ever to have opened a Mexican restaurant in Manhattan, Los Panchos. That was a time when the Upper West Side was still pioneer territory and panting for the refried beans and enchiladas. Oh, Alphie had a grand time with his Mexican restaurant and he, his own boss, could saunter up the block to see Lynn, his wife, and their baby girl, Alison. When a magazine gave the restaurant a review that was between enthusiastic and rave Alphie didn't know what hit him. Yuppies stormed the place and brought their mothers. Under the awning in the back lovers quaffed their Coronas and plighted their troth. Alphie was riding high and why not? He could have been a solicitor in Dublin but he escaped. All he had to do was pass a few exams and appear before the board which would determine if he was respectable enough and intelligent enough to enter the exalted world of Irish law. But what Alphie quickly realized was, yes, it isn't what you know it's who you know and there's a streak of integrity in my brother that erupts in a kiss-my-arse attitude.

If my brother Michael doesn't hold the record for having served more drinks than anyone in the world then he must be close to it. He polished his craft at various New York bars till he was invited to work at Chez Jay in Los Angeles, a hangout for stars and those who like to gaze. Next stop, San Francisco, Perry's on Union Street, a New York–style bar, trendy, with-it, swinging, none of which could describe Mike, who, if he had a mind to, could turn wine into vinegar with one withering look. Many a customer squirmed under the withering look, people who would ask for those exotic drinks that consume a bartender's time and patience. Mike would tell them the candy store was around the corner. If Herb Caen needed something for his column all he had to do was visit Mike and there was enough material for four columns. After a few years there isn't much you can tell a bartender. He hears all the jokes, all the opinions on politics, religion, sex, the stock market. And he grows weary. Mike was recently asked where he'd like to be on the last day of the century. "Home," he said. He'd like to have a nice dinner with wife and family, and what more can a man ask?

When my mother had me she must have been dissatisfied, because a year, a month, and a day later she had Malachy. He was gorgeous—and there were pictures to prove it: reddish blond hair, blue eyes, pink cheeks, pearls for teeth, a personality that would charm Joseph Stalin. When he came to America in 1952 he was like the rest of us: he didn't know what to do with himself. But there were smart people around who spotted the power of that personality and when you combine it with the Irish charm (sorry, Malachy, this is for public consumption) what else can you do but open a bar with Malachy's name on the canopy and Malachy at the door or behind the bar greeting, charming, singing? What else? Producers prowl the bars of New York and spot Malachy and in a minute he's on national TV with Jack Paar, Dick Cavett, Merv Griffin, Mike Douglas, Johnny Carson. They're mad for him the way he brightens the screen and every room he enters. Man, the party doesn't start till Malachy roars in, singing. A dinner table is a dull place without his bon mots, his songs. He's made a dozen movies, acted in plays, read short stories at Symphony Space in New York, written a book, *A Monk Swimming*, available at all fine bookstores. He's been a father five times and there's no end to the grandchildren popping into the world.

There's no end to anything in this family, especially when we're all talking about each other, two about two, three about one.

Or one about three, which is what I've done here.

The McCourts: Malachy, 67; Michael, 62; Alphie, 58; Frank, 68
Photographed by Micheal McLaughlin under the Manhattan
Bridge in Brooklyn, November 11, 1998.

Portfolio III

The Surfing Paskowitzes: from left, Big Moses, 33; Jonathan, 38; Salvador, 30; Joshua Ben, 22; Adam, 32; David, 39; Abraham, 35; Izzy, 34

The eight sons (and one daughter) of surfing legend Doc Paskowitz grew up sharing living space in a twenty-foot-long camper near the beach in San Clemente, California. Izzy, a former world-champion long-boarder, now runs the Paskowitz Surf Camp, where all eleven family members still see one another daily. "My mom went through all the boys, trying to have a daughter, and that was the biggest reason there were so many of us, because we weren't girls," Izzy says. "Joshua was a mistake, but there would have been twenty sons if there hadn't been a daughter."

Photographed by Dorian Caster in San Clemente, California, March 1, 1998.

Albert Belle, 31, baseball player, and his twin, Terrence Belle, 31, financial analyst

"We're very competitive in our fields but not against each other. We just competed against our own goals. I learned at an early age that Albert was blessed with certain talents, and he should do more because he had more talent, and combined with his hard work, he should have more respect. I had talent also, but as far as competing on an equal level, that couldn't be done, because he was better." —**Terrence Belle**

Photographed by John Huet in Chicago, Illinois, January 30, 1998.

Miles Copeland, 54, record company owner; Stewart Copeland, 46, musician, composer; Ian Copeland, 49, booking agent, restaurateur

"We've worked well together because we've all chosen one business to be in, but we've chosen different aspects of that business. The differences between us have become our advantages, they complement one another." —Miles Copeland

Photographed by Matthew Welch in Sherman Oaks, California, January 8, 1999.

Roger Clinton, 41, entertainer; Bill Clinton, 51, President
"In the hours before my most recent State of the Union Address, Roger pulled me aside and handed me a silver dollar that had been our mother's. I carried that coin with me to the podium, knowing that I was carrying the love and support of a strong family and a terrific brother." —**Bill Clinton**

Photographed by Harry Benson in the Cabinet Room of the White House, March 21, 1998.

Phil Guy, 58, blues musician; Buddy Guy, 62, blues musician; Sam Guy, 60, chef

"There always was a lot of music in the family. Our sister sang in the church choir, and sometimes on weekends we had fish fries and Buddy and Phil sat around on the woodpile and played. They'd make guitars out of screen wire, and other folks would come, some sorts of cousins of ours, and they'd all play together. All acoustic, none of the electric guitars they're playing now." —**Sam Guy**

Photographed by Bill Phelps at Buddy Guy's Legends in Chicago, Illinois, January 30, 1999.

Austin and Luke Brown, twins, on their sixth birthday

"I like sharing my birthday with my brother. He's good company." —**Austin Brown**

"We got the same presents. I wish my birthday was on a different day.
We can get different presents that way." —**Luke Brown**

Photographed by Brian Velenchenko at the Discovery Zone, Annapolis Maryland, March 28, 1998.

Hank Buchanan, 60, accountant; Jack Buchanan, 50, accountant; Pat Buchanan, 59, pundit;
Brian Buchanan, 47, doctor; Tom Buchanan, 44, lawyer; James Buchanan, 57, dentist

"Brotherhood tends to mitigate against the idea that you're some special, privileged individual. There was an awful lot of fights, sure. But it's mainly that you defend one another against the outside." —Pat Buchanan

Photographed by Nitin Vadukul at CNN's Washington Bureau, March 31, 1998.

Tom and Terry Brands, 30, wrestlers

Growing up in Sheldon, Iowa, twin brothers Tom and Terry Brands spent most of their free time in the family's basement, where there was a small wrestling mat. "We'd have duals," Terry recalls. "I'd be the Russians, and Tommy'd be the Americans, and we'd wrestle six-minute matches, all ten weight classes. It taught us to wrestle in the center of the mat. Those walls were awful hard."

Photographed by Kurt Markus in the Carver-Hawkeye Arena at the University of Iowa in Iowa City, February 24, 1999.

The brothers of NASCAR
back row: Geoff Bodine, 49; Todd Bodine, 34; and Brett Bodine, 39
middle row: Mark Green, 39; David Green, 40; Elliott Sadler, 23; Jeff Burton, 31; Ward Burton, 37;
Rusty Wallace, 42; Kenny Wallace, 42; Michael Waltrip, 35; front row: Jeff Green, 36; Hermie Sadler, 29;
Terry Labonte, 41; Darrell Waltrip, 51; Bobby Labonte, 34

Photographed by David Harry Stewart in victory lane at the Atlanta Motor Speedway, November 6, 1998.

POLE DAY
NOV. 6, 1998

risking my dink

Rosemary Mahoney

My mother had seven children in seven years: four girls, three boys. I was the youngest. We grew up in a house at the edge of the woods. There was a stream behind it that fed into a marsh, and beyond that a corn field that was rimmed with rib-high timothy grass that released a fountain of crickets and bugs when you walked through it and left stripes of green on your bare legs. The top floor of our house was divided by a central staircase into the boys' half and the girls' half. Each half had its own large playroom flanked by a row of tiny bedrooms—cells really—big enough for a bed, a desk, a bureau. The boys' bedrooms were papered with scenes from America's colonial history (Penn's Treaty with the Indians, Washington's Delaware Crossing, Franklin's Experiment, Paul Revere's Ride), navigational tools and charts, famously adventurous seafaring men with swords on their hips, celestial constellations, directional compass roses, whales and ships, eagles symbolic of liberty, the various forms of nautical knots—they were surrounded with information, interest, historical human influence, pictures suggestive of the wide world beyond our house. On the other side of the house, the girls' bedrooms were papered with a pretty floral print suggestive of . . . well, prettiness.

I loved my three sisters. When one of them sewed her own clothes on the sewing machine, or delighted in the hundred ways you could prepare an eggplant, I admired her ingenuity and skill, tried on the dress she'd made, ate the eggplant with interest, but was never inspired to imitate those activities. Another sister, at fifteen, spent a great deal of time having political impulses and improving her hair, mixing raw eggs and essence of fresh lemons into her shampoo; she complained bitterly about the U.S. government and the military in Vietnam. The third sister, Ellen, the one closest to me in age, was interested in animals, had a cat who lived with its kittens in a drawer of her bureau, and was fascinated by the newspaper, particularly the stories recounting kidnappings and murders. My sisters babysat and knitted and braided bracelets out of gimp. They were also athletic, rode their bicycles all over town, schemed, skated well, played on sports teams at school, occasionally fought with each other, were territorial about their bedrooms, and liked prowling in the woods and diverting the stream to create a little swimming hole. I could talk to my sisters freely. If I said some impulsive spontaneous thing, they wouldn't suddenly sneer, "Will you shut up, idiot!" the way my brothers might, or repeat what I had said in a whining voice that made me seem petty and ridiculous. They were protective and forbearing; I was one of them and felt safe in their presence. They were different from my brothers: they were unconditionally nice to me.

And yet it was true that if I found myself engaged in some pursuit with my sisters and happened to hear the shouts of my brothers playing somewhere else, I was driven by pure desire to drop what I was doing and join them. If I had the choice—and I often did—I chose to be with my brothers. They played mumblety-peg with a switchblade one of them had cunningly acquired in Boston, popped wheelies up and down the driveway on their bicycles, set up a bicycle jump in the back yard and flung themselves over it again and again. They concocted gasoline bombs under the back porch. They watched Saturday morning wrestling—fat, grunting, double-chinned men in leotards grimacing stagily and butting their jiggling bellies together—then went outside to try for themselves what they'd seen. (Stephen once broke Johnny's arm practicing a particularly hokey half-nelson.) They conducted carefully orchestrated rock fights, water balloon fights, fights with tightly rolled wet tea towels expertly flicked against patches of vulnerably exposed flesh. James, at fifteen, had a real bullwhip and a morose boa constrictor that swallowed live mice whole in a vivid and lewd and broodingly prolonged display of peristalsis. Stephen had a stash of itching powder from Jack's Joke Shop, and Johnny had a BB gun that he used to shoot out the rear window of my mother's station wagon. When Johnny got hit by a car while riding his bicycle, the bicycle was demolished, but he walked away to tell, in jaunty detail, the glorious story. In snowstorms all three of my brothers grabbed onto the rear bumpers of cars slowly making the turn from one snowy street to the next and, in a cloud of carbon monoxide, skied up the street behind them on their leather-soled engineer boots, seeing who could hold on the longest.

There was a risky cleverness in the schemes my brothers came up with, a death-defying esprit de corps. They had a genius for testing their own limits, a willingness to risk pain and failure to find out how much their hearts and bodies could give. Or take. To them the world was a competition, a quest to see who could live the most. My sisters, who took pride enough in their various skills, didn't seem to care this deeply about winning. But I cared. I wanted desperately to be in the middle of whatever fray my brothers had cooked up, to be tough enough to keep up with them. There was, it seemed, something crucially at stake in their pitiless and intense way of playing, something to do with seizing life, with flouting death.

I learned to play street hockey with my brothers. I wanted to play over at Milton Academy with my brother Johnny and his friends, but first I had to prove myself, prove that I would-n't embarrass him by crying or screwing up. I knew that if I did either he would kill me. I'd seen this happen to my friend Mary. The kids in our neighborhood were engaged in a particularly violent rock fight when she was struck on the wrist by a rock her brother had thrown. She began to cry and, worse, to threaten to tell her mother, which made me cringe with its appalling lack of forethought. The sweating brother went rigid and roared at her with the authority of an SS officer, "Shut up, Mary, or I'll pull your dink off!" Somewhere in the muddy recesses of his mind the brother must have known that in Mary's case there was, in fact, no dink to be pulled off, but in the savagery of the rock fight, the dink and its obliteration was what was important. In that ruthless world the issue was: a dink for a dink. My dink or yours.

Johnny and I practiced upstairs in the playroom, whipping pucks against the wall, slap shots, wrist shots, dribbling, taking splinters from the wide floorboards in the soles of our stockinged feet. Johnny was nearly two years older than I and in certain moods might pound me against the refrigerator just for looking at him. He could call me "douche bag" and "moron," "cunt face" and "idiot" and twist my arm behind my back or hurl a ski pole at me with such harpooning force that it punctured first the fabric of my jeans and then the flesh of my thigh, astonishing both of us, and then half an hour later, forgetting him-self, he would tell me I knew how to ride a bike better than Ted Putnam and that I was the best pitcher he had ever seen.

One bright April Saturday morning I asked him if I could come and play street hockey with him. He shrugged and said, "I don't give a shit," which was as close as he ever got to saying yes, then he rode off to the game on his bicycle without telling me he was leaving. I glimpsed him from the living room window pedaling off down our driveway and ran for my hockey stick, a cracked Koho he had cast off, and raced after him on my bike, slamming in and out of potholes, straining to keep, through the fuzz of new buds on the trees, sight of Johnny. He was way ahead of me, a small dot furiously peddling, his bicycle slightly too big for him and his body tilting from side to side as he stretched to keep his toes on the pedals. I thought I saw him turn and look back at me, but it could have been anything he was looking at.

My bike was a pink and white Schwinn Princess, too small for me, with fat tires and white plastic hand grips and no gears, a prissy little bicycle that had been passed down through a sister or two. The rubber parts of the pedals had long since broken off, and I had to place my feet on the remaining metal bars, which were bent in the middle like horse bits and hurt my feet through the thin soles of my sneakers. With each rotation of the pedal, the bicycle cried out like a hound in pain. I wanted a bike like Johnny's, with a banana seat and rabbit-ear handlebars.

In the parking lot behind the Milton Academy girls' school, the boys gathered for the hockey game, and when he saw me the biggest one, Jackie Smith, said to Johnny with grinning skepticism, "Mahoney, that's your sister."

The look on Johnny's face said *No shit* as he stared at Jackie Smith. Johnny was pale, and thin, and if you had never witnessed the way he threw a baseball, or skated backwards, or ran from here to there with liquid agility, or scrambled squirrel-like over a chain-link fence, you might have been deceived into thinking he was vulnerable and weak and possibly girlish. His black hair was longish, hovering in sideswept bangs over his brow, and invariably he showed up to play street hockey in brown oxfords with leather soles, the stodgy, downtrodden shoes of a failed salesman. Up and down his bare skinny shins he had scars and gouges and the red welts of flea bites. He was small and tough and the best athlete among us, and none of the other kids ever questioned him.

"My sister's playin'," Johnny said.

I could tell that the street hockey game had gone well if Johnny didn't punch me afterwards. Back at home, sitting beside him on my mother's bed, happily watching the one TV in our house, I stayed warily on guard, expecting a sudden slap or slug at any moment, or for him to turn and say, "Hi, fuckface" when I hadn't uttered a word. That day, he didn't punch me. He was sitting beside me, absorbed in whatever TV show we were watching— *F-Troop*, maybe, or *The Three Stooges*. His obliviousness to me was a kind of acceptance. I'd passed the test.

Only now, almost thirty years after the fact, can I confess this: Once I snuck Johnny's mini-bike out of the cellar and rode it up and down our long driveway for two hours while he was at a friend's house. I knew I was risking my dink when I did that. The consequences would have been severe if he had caught me riding—or for that matter, standing anywhere near—his beloved mini-bike. Had he known, Johnny would have crucified me in his own manner: pinned me down on the floor, slapped my head, stuffed my own long hair into my mouth and across my eyes, and drooled on my face until I screamed and eventually burst into tears that I couldn't contain. And if I cried he would crown the torture by imitating my crying with an eery and infuriating accuracy, his face mockingly twisted into a slit-eyed Greek mask of tragedy. But the draw to try the mini-bike was too strong. It was bright red, with fat knobby tires and a soft black leather seat. I knew how to start it, because a hundred times I had watched him do it. When I twisted the accelerator handle the machine responded with a fervid little leap, like a live animal, and yet the propulsive surge was oddly like an expression, an extension, of my own will. I could feel my heart beating in my throat as I went off down the driveway, fearful at first, starting and stopping, testing the brake, my feet gently grazing the ground like two dragging anchors and my ponytailed head snapping backward with each erratic twist of the handle. Jerkily I proceeded until I got the hang of it, and then I went faster. And then I went fast. Down to the end of the road and back again, as fast as I could, stirring up pebbles, the wind just brisk enough to rattle my cheeks and whip tears into my eyes and fling a fly to its death against the hurtling wall of my forehead. I could feel the heat of the muffler warming my right ankle. The tiny engine gave off a bleating whine that Johnny would have been able to hear a quarter of a mile away. I felt like I was flying, and I figured if I went fast enough, was maybe just a little bit lucky, I might even get away with it.

a ton of muscle

Thomas Kelly

There is something not just old school but Old World about the McCabes. It is easy to picture them as the guys sent out by the chieftain to tear the livers out of interlopers, to defend the tribe from all corners. They evoke a time when you created a large brood out of mean necessity. They are a burly bunch. A few years back, before the two oldest—Frankie and Terry—died, they amounted to about a ton of muscle. Today, the six surviving brothers (another, Dennis, died as an infant) are gathered to mark the sixteenth anniversary of the passing of their father, a man who raised them and four sisters on a barman's wages. I can imagine the feed bill.

We are back in the old neighborhood, which lies at the ass end of the A train in South Jamaica, Queens. It's a red-brick and blue-collar part of New York, long beyond the spill of Manhattan's shadow. This is where, thirty years ago, they played street hockey and stickball and football and boxed and served Mass and brawled and ducked nuns' knuckles and outran cops and chased girls and careened off one another within their tight-knit world. It's the place that tempered them into men.

The McCabes:
Brian, 42, NYPD detective; Joe, 39,
teamster; Peter, 44, construction
supervisor; Kevin, 46, political campaign manager; Gerard, 39, attorney;
Timmy, 47, mechanical engineer
*Photographed by Micheal McLaughlin
in Queens, March 15, 1998.*

The McCabes pepper the chill spring air with insults. It is good-natured ball breaking that ricochets around and leaves none unscathed. The location leads to reminiscence, and most of the stories are about times they had on this corner. More than a few are about scuffles and skirmishes that occurred before fistfighting died as a New York City art form. Once, when one of the twins was waylaid by the scions of some local wiseguys, word shot through the neighborhood. McCabes started coming and kept on coming till one of the deflated wannabes whined, "Hey, how many brothers you got?"

These days, they are too busy for street fights. There is family—the clan has provided Mom with forty-five grandchildren and seventeen great-grandchildren—and there is work. The McCabe brothers constitute the sinew of the city. Joe, thirty-nine, is a teamster who hustles cargo in and out of JFK; Gerard (Joe's twin) is a firefighter turned prosecutor turned defense lawyer; Brian, forty-two, is an NYPD detective who lassos perps in Hell's Kitchen; Peter, forty-four, is a construction supervisor; Kevin, forty-six, is a political campaign manager and former chief of staff for the city council; and Timmy, forty-seven, is a mechanical engineer who rehabs public schools. In this transient age, all but one still live in the county of their birth.

As they mill about this morning, waiting for the photographer to snap their picture, their cohesion is tangible. It's as if they were less a group of individuals than a single being, as if their hand-me-down youth distilled the notion of brotherhood to a purer grain. I ask Brian what happens if one of them is in trouble, and he states simply, "You get the phone call, you go. You don't ask questions." Just the thought of these McCabes moving in one direction with bad intent is enough to make you pray you are not in the way.

the scarlet ibis

Tom Junod

I never get tired when I'm running with my brother. I never even get winded. I stride, and I kick, and the faster I run, the stronger I get. No matter how hard I try, however, I can never push past him—I can never put distance between us. We run together, stride for stride, shoulder to shoulder, as though attached by a tether, and sometimes I get light-headed, with the exhilaration of it—with the feeling of exclusion; with the feeling of simultaneous freedom and constraint; with the feeling that the world is narrowing around us, even as it opens, and opening, even as it closes in. It's addictive, this sensation, and it's what drives our final, greedy kick, when I can hear our twinned heels turning up gravel on the pathway, and I feel as though we're flying down a tunnel, toward some light-strewn clearing that will remain just beyond us, always a step away. Indeed, I always have a sense of *inevitability* when I'm running with my brother—of consequence—as though each of our strides is in some way decisive, and when we finally stop I always make the silent boast of barely breathing, though I can feel the tickle of my heart in my chest.

I don't get this feeling with anyone else. I have *never* gotten this feeling with anyone else, because I'm not what is called a good runner, and neither is my brother. We both labor. I'm that disheartening combination, skinny and slow. I ran track in high school for one season, and was too plodding for sprints and too lacking in lung power for distance, and so ran the quarter-mile, and puked at the end of every race. As for my brother Michael—my big brother Michael—well, he is not so skinny as I am, and maybe not so slow, but he is ten years older than me, and two years ago, when he was just forty-eight, he had his chest cracked open for a triple bypass, and under his running shirt, he still wears, like a burn, like a brand, the shiny purplish scar.

When I was still in grade school, I had a favorite short story. It was called, if I remember correctly, "The Scarlet Ibis," and it was about two brothers. One was older—or, in the nomenclature of brotherhood, "big"—and one younger, or "little." The little brother's name was Doodle. He was small and sickly, and he had a weak heart, as the result of some post-natal fever, possibly scarlet. The story was the big brother's to tell, with longing and rue. He was bigger than Doodle in every way—bigger and stronger, with a heart that never betrayed him. Although he loved Doodle very much, he was also puzzled—embarrassed—by his weakness, and sought to *improve* him, by making him run. He believed that Doodle could get better, if only he *wanted* to get better, and so every day he took his little brother out to the road in front of their house, and under the prod of a stopwatch, demanded that Doodle run faster and farther, until his face blazed with strain, and was as red as the plumage of the freakish tropical bird that shadowed Doodle wherever he went, the scarlet ibis. For a while, the big brother's plan seemed to work, for Doodle kept running faster and farther, but then big brother got greedy—he seemed to believe he was *creating* Doodle, as he improved him—and wanted Doodle to enter a race, to prove the power of his own program. Doodle didn't want to, and so, one day, to punish him, the brother dropped Doodle off in the middle of nowhere, and made him run home, underneath the black clouds of a gathering storm. Doodle was terrified of being alone, and so he trudged along, in tears, until he saw the scarlet ibis, stricken or shot dead by the side of the road, and it started to rain. And then he began to run. He ran faster and faster, in the awful freedom of the terrible storm, until he achieved some kind of ecstasy. And his heart burst. When his brother went out into the rain to look for him, he found him face down by the side of the road, soaking wet. He thought that Doodle was slacking—that he had given up. He turned Doodle over, and saw that he had a smile on his face, but that the blood gushing from his nose had turned his face and his entire body a hue of crimson. He was dead, and now, at last, his brother knew that *Doodle* was the scarlet ibis, fragile and freakish and irreconcilable to the brother's notion of strength and normality. So there. The end.

We always ran together, Michael and I—he always *made* me run, from the time I was a toddler, and he, as my baby-sitter, dispatched me on incessant laps of the living room, to tire me out. We ran on the beach, and we ran in the streets of our hometown, for some reason almost always at night, and one time, as I tagged along ten yards behind him, a dog came snarling out of the darkness and my brother appeared, as though out of nowhere, and interposed himself between me and the sharpened bones of those snapping jaws. He was my protector, you see—almost a father, as much as he was a brother. We weren't competitive, the way some brothers are—or, at least we didn't acknowledge the competition between us, if only because competition demands equivalent contestants, and we both knew all too well who held the vanquishing hand. It wasn't that I was afraid of Michael— I never was, for he never gave me reason to be. It was simply that I neither would nor could rise up against him, although the first Christmas gift I remember getting from him was a pair of boxing gloves adorned with reproductions of Rocky Marciano's signature, and the moment I laced them on I tilted at him with windmill punches that lifted me off the floor, my fists curled in gloves as hard as cured concrete. I was no more than six, or seven, or eight; he was sixteen, or seventeen, or eighteen, and he endured my frantic, flailing charges until at last he tapped me in the nose with a series of soft jabs, and I retired, in anger and frustration and probably in tears.

I say all of this without resentment—or with as little resentment as possible— because it has always been a little miracle of my life that my brother and I have loved one another so openly, so deeply, despite the difference in our ages. Indeed, for a very long time, I not only idolized Michael, but aspired to complete some kind of twinship with him, although he was already a twin, fraternally, with my sister, Cathy. I used to want to butt in, on my brother and sister's twinship—I used to think I could do it *better* than they could, and was disappointed when anybody failed to notice the resemblance between my brother and myself. I reasoned that Michael and I were twins, born ten years apart, and it was not until my sister pulled me aside and told me something I hated to hear—told me how obvious it was, that I was trying to live my life in paltry imitation of my brother, told me that it was time I became my own man—that I started forming myself as a person. I became obsessed with the sport that allowed me to slide outside the patronage of Michael's shadow—I was already starting to become obsessed with football.

My brother did not play football. I did. Though not overly skilled, I was fanatical about it, and tried to incorporate my fanaticism into my game, dreaming of becoming a receiver on the order of Raymond Berry or Freddy Biletnikoff—a pass-catcher who worried himself into greatness, who bit his nails to gain greater feel for the ball, who slathered his socks with stickum, who ran disciplined patterns, who was slow and dependable, who caught *everything*. Mike thought that I was *too* slow—he thought I should be quarterback, to take advantage of my brains, and to that end he took me to a football field, where he stood on a stripe ten yards away, and asked me to throw him the ball. I couldn't reach him. Again and again, I threw him the ball, and again and again the ball hit the ground before hitting his hands, until I gave up. I walked off the field, in utter defeat, utter dejection, but my brother put his arm around me and told me not to quit—and so I didn't. Although I know how corny this all sounds, I came back the next day and the next, and I threw the ball to whoever would catch it. Four years later, in the summer before my senior year in high school, I could throw a football about sixty yards, which believe me, is a very long way. I was about to start a season in which I actually started as quarterback in a few games, and threw a handful of touchdown passes. I was lifting weights. I was *strong*, and went out to prove it to my brother—went out to prove to him what Doodle could do.

He was married, by then, and one night, just after sundown, we drove from his apartment to a football field, and began to run. We started slow, as we always do—we "jogged." Then we sped up. He was twenty-seven, and I was seventeen, and we ran about five miles, at full gallop, into the late-summer darkness, and for the first time in each of our lives, we were neck and neck. We each ran as hard as we could, and yet no matter how hard we tried, we couldn't extricate ourselves from one another. I couldn't outrun him, and he couldn't outrun me, and that's how we stayed, until the end—two boys, two men, suddenly *stuck* with each other, hitting the stretch at full stride, so exhausted that we could taste the blood in our lungs, and yet giddy with some kind of tingling delight, with the sensation of being fearless out there on the precipice of arrival. I mean, I remember how *funny* the whole thing was, or became, I remember that we started *laughing* in our final kick, at the comedy of each other's will, of each other's determination to be indomitable; and I remember thinking that before I gave my brother or myself any quarter, I would rather have died.

He is fifty now, and I am forty. We started running together again two months after he got his bypass. It scared me, how much he struggled at first—how heavy his steps were, how stiff his stride—and I used to ask him, all the time, "How are you feeling, Bro'? You okay? Do you want to slow down?" Still, even then, I had to remind myself to be careful, because my natural inclination was to speed up, in answer to the strength I felt surging through me, the ease that had overtaken my stride. Then one day, weeks, maybe months later, I let myself go out ahead of him, just to do it, just because I *could*, and he followed—or, rather, he never let me get away, and ran next to me the whole time, huffing and puffing, with a slick of sweat on his forehead. "You okay?" "Yeah, I'm fine." We have run next to each other ever since, one or two times a week, sometimes fast, sometimes slow, sometimes *starting* slow, until we catch fire, and our legs get greedy, and we go. We'll be talking about the same things we always talk about—the things we talk about so incessantly that it might seem we've run out of things to say, when precisely the opposite is true—namely, the relative merits of *Breaking Away* (his movie) versus those of *Dazed and Confused* (mine), and then his job, his family, his health, his troubles. We rarely talk about me, and sometimes, as though to account for myself, I'll find myself picking up speed where the path narrows and is overhung by a winnowing canopy of trees. I'll find myself *competing* with him, although neither of us has ever said a single word about the competition between us, and although it is at these ruthlessly brisk moments that I remember how I've neglected to learn CPR, as though still living on the faith that my big brother will never fall down. It will always be getting dark when we start our race. It will always be last light, or light so weak it's turning blue, and so neither he nor I ever consider stopping, because the world is rushing past us and we're rushing past the world, and we're flying together down some tunnel toward some place we've never been. In all my life, I've never had to ask my brother for anything, I don't think; I've never really *bothered* him for anything, but now my body will venture a silent question, and my legs will make an unvoiced demand; we'll be running together, as we always have, and as an almost unwelcome strength gathers inside me, and I feel myself surging toward an almost unwanted freedom, what I'll be whispering to him is this: Kick, my brother, *kick*—and please don't let me pass you by.

Portfolio IV

Richard A. Jones, 48, state Superior Court judge; Quincy Jones, 65, producer, arranger, musician, composer
"We're so close because we're very independent—we both work in our own tracks. Quincy has always respected people who are independent and creative, who work and do things on their own, have earned success on their own right, paid their dues." —**Richard Jones**

Photographed by Fergus Greer in Bel Air, California, February 8, 1999.

Thomas Blake, Jr., 22, professional tennis player; James Blake, 19, top-ranked college tennis player

Photographed by Michael Lavine at Harvard University's Beren Tennis Center in Cambridge, Massachusetts, February 23, 1999.

John Foley, 35, UPS account manager; Mankind (Mick Foley), 33, professional wrestler

"This book is probably the first thing we've had in common since the Christmas morning Yorkshire pudding eating contests—he always gave me a run for my money, but I always won." —**Mankind**

Photographed by Matt Petosa at Nassau Coliseum in Uniondale, New York, March 30, 1999.

David Lee, 37, photographer; Cinque Lee, 31, filmmaker; Spike Lee, 41, filmmaker

"My parents placed more responsibilities on me because I was the oldest. I was expected to take care of my siblings—it was as simple as that. It's just funny being the oldest and seeing everybody grow up, because a lot of times I can remember changing their diapers, and now they're grown men." —**Spike Lee**

Photographed by John Huet at Sun Studios in New York City, February 26, 1998.

Joseph Dunand, 34, retailer and graduate student; Alex Rodriguez, 23, baseball player

"We've always been into sports. When he was a kid, he was trying to compete against me. When he was five years old he was trying to beat me in basketball, and I would trash him like 52–0, and he would be sore and upset that he couldn't beat me. That propelled him to want to compete, so when he played against kids his own age he would be so much better than them. The first time he came to the Dominican Republic—he was about ten—he never touched a football in his life and we went out to the park and tried to play three on three with some other guys. I threw him a bomb and he caught it over a high school guy. I was surprised and amazed, and ever since then he's never stopped amazing me." —**Joseph Dunand**

Photographed by Davis Factor at the Seattle Mariners' spring training camp in Peoria, Arizona, March 6, 1999.

Richard Butler, 42, musician, painter; Tim Butler, 40, musician
Photographed by Brian Velenchenko at Dodge Studio in New York City, January 5, 1999.

Joe Mullen, 41 and Brian Mullen, 36, hockey players

Growing up in Hell's Kitchen on the far west side of Midtown Manhattan, Joe and Brian Mullen gave a new meaning to "mean streets." With every free minute, they played street hockey on the New York Printing School blacktop across the street from their Forty-ninth Street apartment—the street where this photo was taken.

"We were always out there," says Joe Mullen. "It didn't matter how cold it was or what time of the year, we would have a game going."

The two went on to become a great success story in American ice hockey. After finally getting the chance to play on ice in their teen years, Joe went on to a Hall-of-Fame NHL career and still holds the record for the most goals and points for an American-born player. Brian was an All-Star defensive forward, his career cut short in 1993 by a variety of health problems.

In 1995, the brothers together received the Lester Patrick Award, the highest American honor in hockey. And these days both are still active in the sport. Joe has recently played on the USA Hockey qualifying team and works in the Pittsburgh Penguins front office. Brian promotes hockey, both on the ice and off, for the NHL.

Photographed by Harry Benson on Forty-ninth Street in New York City, December 23, 1998.

Four generations of Swans: John B. Swan, 100, and Tom Swan, 92; Tom Swan, Jr., 70, and Robert Swan, 61; Kevin Swan, 45, and Steven Swan, 41; Ryan Swan, 13, and Greg Swan, 7

The Swan brothers all live within a hundred miles of one another, just west of the Delaware River in Pennsylvania. The family traces its roots back to William Swan, who left England aboard the *True Love* and landed in Salem, Massachusetts, in 1632. Today, Kevin (the son of Tom Jr. and the father of Ryan and Greg) designs computer systems for the space-shuttle program.

"When Steve and I were young," Kevin says, "we did different things, maybe on purpose. I see that with my sons, too. Ryan played a lot of baseball and soccer, but he doesn't do that anymore, because those are Greg's sports now."

Kevin's father likes to remind them that they are all the descendants of colonial silversmiths, Congressmen, and the occasional horse thief.

"The Swan brothers, we all have a very dry, very wry sense of humor," Kevin says. "I think it drives our wives nuts."

Photographed by Andrea Modica at the Willow Valley Manor, outside Lancaster, Pennsylvania, April 3, 1998.

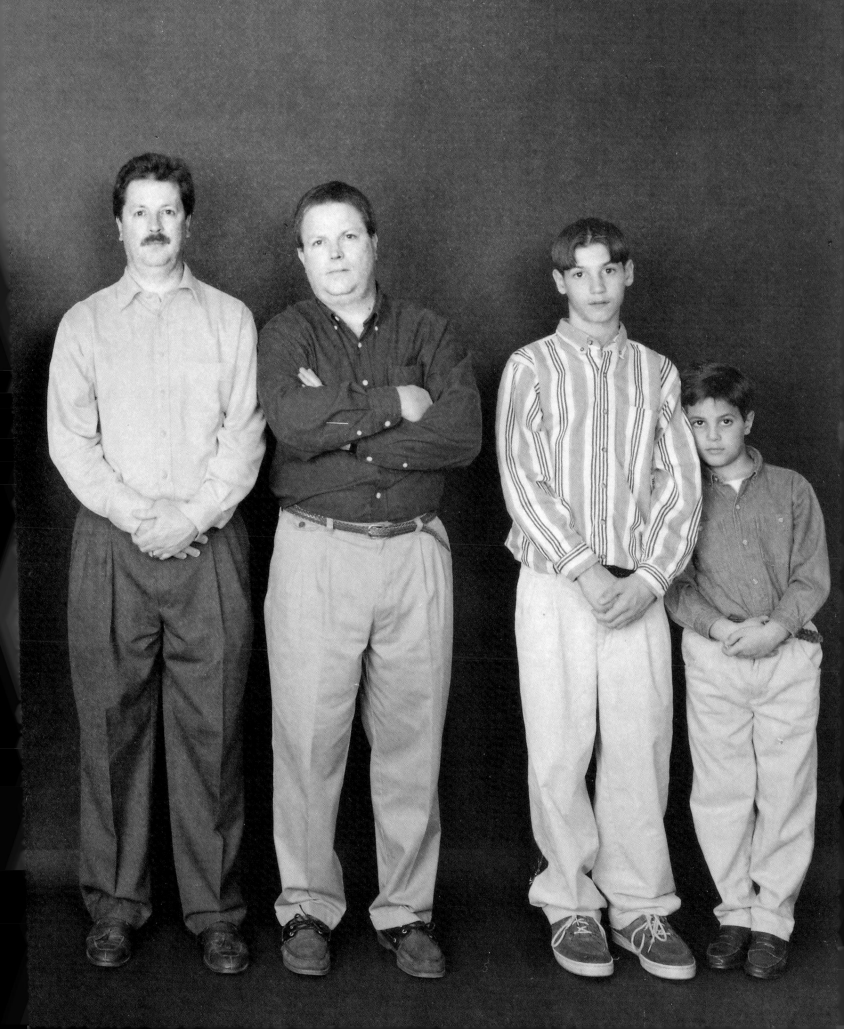

Contributors

Scott Anderson is the author, most recently, of *The Man Who Tried to Save the World* and *Triage*, a novel. He co-authored *Inside the League* and *War Zones* with his brother, Jon Lee Anderson.

Larry Doyle, a former editor of *National Lampoon, Spy,* and *New York Magazine,* is a writer on *The Simpsons.*

Richard Ford is the author of many acclaimed works of fiction, including *Rock Springs, The Sportswriter,* and *Independence Day,* which received the Pulitzer Prize.

Tom Junod, an *Esquire* writer-at-large, is the only writer ever to win back-to-back National Magazine Awards for feature writing.

Thomas Kelly is a frequent contributor to *Esquire* and author of the novel *Payback.*

Thomas A. Kelley, a former Peace Corps volunteer in Niger, is an associate professor at the University of North Carolina Law School.

Joseph P. Kennedy II, a former Congressman from Massachusetts, is the founder and chief executive of Citizens Energy in Boston.

Frank McCourt is the author of *'Tis,* a sequel to the Pulitzer Prize-winning memoir *Angela's Ashes.*

James Alan McPherson received the Pulitzer Prize for his second collection of stories, *Elbow Room.* He is the author, most recently, of *Crabcakes,* a memoir.

Rosemary Mahoney is the author of three books of nonfiction, most recently the memoir *A Likely Story: One Summer with Lillian Hellman.*

Mark O'Donnell is a novelist and former writer for *Saturday Night Live.*

Steve O'Donnell has been a television writer for numerous shows, including *Chris Rock, Lateline,* and *David Letterman.*

Charles P. Pierce is a writer-at-large for *Esquire* and the author of a forthcoming family memoir about Alzheimer's.

Scott Raab is a writer-at-large at *Esquire*.

David Sedaris is an *Esquire* contributing editor and the best-selling author of *Holidays on Ice*, *Naked*, and *Barrel Fever*.

Tobias Wolff is the author of *This Boy's Life*, *In Pharoh's Army*, and several collections of short stories, most recently *The Night in Question*.

Credits

PAGE 23:
Styling by Randi Packard for Tiffany Whitford, New York.

Martin's suit by Giorgio Armani; Frank's suit by Paul Stuart; shirts, ties, and belts by Giorgio Armani.

PAGE 24:
Grooming by Mary Klimek; Styling by Rita Rago.

PAGES 26-7:
Grooming by Charlene Roberson; Styling by Daniel Caudill for Visages Style.

PAGE 29:
Grooming by Barbara Farman for Cloutier; Prop styling by Shannon Shapiro for Artist Group Management.

PAGE 63:
Grooming by Nancy Sprague for Mark Edward, Inc.

PAGES 66-7:
Grooming by Susan Haddon for Celestine; Styling by Albert Mendonca for Celestine.

PAGE 85:
Grooming by Max Pinnell for Bumble and Bumble, New York.

PAGE 96:

Styling by Christy Grecco; Grooming by Nick Harris; Albert's suit by Kenneth Cole, shirt by Perry Ellis, tie by Mondo; Terrence's suit by Kenneth Cole, shirt by Perry Ellis, tie by Geoffrey Beane.

PAGE 97:

Grooming by Lynn Taylor for Rex.

PAGES 120-1:

Grooming by Dawn Haines.

PAGE 124:

Grooming by Irene Vass for Ennis, Inc.; Styling by Jane Choi for Ennis, Inc.

PAGE 126:

Grooming by Dale Johnson for Tiffany Whitford, New York; Styling by Louise Godwin for Tiffany Whitford, New York.

Richard's knit top by Calvin Klein, pants by Helmut Lang, shoes by Costume National; Tim's jacket by Calvin Klein, sweater by Paul Smith, pants by NY Industrie.

Richard's suit by Costume National, shirt by Calvin Klein, shoes by Costume National; Tim's suit by Hugo Boss, shirt by Costume National.